Dick:

I hope you enjoy
reading this book as much
as I enjoyed writing it.

Best Regards,

Dwight R. Messimer

No Margin for Error

No Margin for Error

THE U.S. NAVY'S TRANSPACIFIC FLIGHT OF 1925

Dwight R. Messimer

NAVAL INSTITUTE PRESS
Annapolis, Maryland

TO RENATE

Printed in the United States of America

Library of Congress Cataloging in Publication Data
Messimer, Dwight R. 1937–
    No margin for error.
Bibliography: p.
Includes index.
1. Transpacific flights.   I.   Title.
TL531.M37   629.13'09153   80–84063
ISBN 0–87021–497–7

Contents

Preface

A story about five men lost at sea for nine days would not seem to be much different than any other story about shipwrecked sailors. But this story is different. These five men were not adrift in an open boat, their tongues swollen from thirst and their bodies burned black by the tropical sun. These men did not stare helplessly at the empty horizon waiting for some sign of rescue, nor did they go mad and commit the bestialities so often described.

These five men, exercising resourcefulness and ingenuity, rigged their vessel with sails, devised a crude method of steering and sailed 450 miles to safety. The remarkable part about the story is that they did all this in a twin-engine, biplane flying boat called *PN9–1*.

The events that put them and their airplane adrift upon the Pacific; how the meticulously prepared plan, intended to prevent just such an event from happening, fell apart at the last minute; the full account of their nine-day ordeal; and the role their ordeal played in saving naval aviation from being absorbed into an independent national air force are told in the following pages.

The author's intent is that this little-known, often ignored event be credited with the historical significance that it deserves. The story is set against the background of General William "Billy" Mitchell's seven-year campaign to establish an independent air force. The twenty-one months during 1923 and 1924 when the Bureau of Aeronautics (BURAERO) was moving slowly toward the west coast—Hawaii flight project are treated only generally. Emphasized instead is the urgency of the project as it was actually carried out, beginning early in 1925. Ultimately, the central theme is the *PN9–1* and her five-man crew.

The reader is urged to consult the reference notes which contain a large amount of data, the inclusion of which in the text would have been cumbersome and distracting.

Acknowledgements

Without the help and support of many people this book could not have been written. I owe thanks to three good friends. Dr. George Moore, Ph.D., read the original manuscript and recommended many important editorial changes. Dr. Gerald Wheeler, Ph.D., provided me with some fine research leads and Dr. Charles Burdick, Ph.D., gave me technical advice. The staff of the Naval Historical Center and the National Archives, Navy and Old Army Branch, went beyond the limits of normal expectations—and even hopes—to dig out documents for me. The people of the Library of Congress were similarly helpful. Special thanks should also go to Kirk Austen for drawing the charts that appear in the book. But the biggest debt is owed to my wife who typed the manuscript in the "final" form so often that she can now say the entire book by rote.

Introduction

The fabric, what little there was, hung in tattered rags from the lower wings. The starboard engine displayed a gaping cavity as though an enormous shark had bitten a chunk out of the nacelle. Debris, a mangled fuel tank, and tangled lines cluttered the hull. Beneath the port engine was a crumpled piece of canvas that looked like a dirty field dressing pressed over a terrible wound.

The caption beneath the old photograph described the biplane as the *PN9–1* and said that the flying boat had survived nine days adrift at sea. To the person who wrote that brief caption, the significance of the event lay in the demonstrated strength of the metal hull. The real importance of the nine-day odyssey, however, lay in the national events that followed it.

Alone, the *PN9–1* would have accounted for little, if any, lasting significance. But fate joined the saga of the *PN9–1* and her crew with two other explosive events that turned the *PN9–1*'s failure to fly nonstop from San Francisco to Hawaii into success. One of these other events was the tragic loss of the dirigible USS *Shenandoah* in September 1925. The other event was Army General William "Billy" Mitchell's reaction to the failure of the *PN9–1* and the crash of the *Shenandoah*. He charged the War and Navy Departments with ". . . criminal negligence and almost treasonable administration. . . ."[1]

Ironically, this coalition of disaster was to have many positive results, one of the most immediate being the end of Mitchell's campaign to incorporate naval aviation into an independent national air force. As it turned out, had any of the three events failed to occur at the time and in the order in which they did, the Navy might have lost its air arm.

In 1919 General Mitchell had entered the list as the self-appointed champion for American aviation and his battle cry

1

was "air power." His goal was not merely to advance Army aviation, he wanted nothing less than an independent national air force responsible for *all* aviation matters in the United States. Mitchell's scheme was, of course, unacceptable to the Navy, and the Army was not overly enthusiastic about having a crusader in its midst who was answering a higher calling.

In an energetic and bombastic campaign, often marked by outrageous, headline-grabbing exaggerations, Mitchell attacked the Navy, which he declared had been made obsolete by military aircraft. Despite his rhetoric, Mitchell was not really after the Battle Fleet. He wanted the Navy's air arm, and by mid-1924 he was very close to achieving his goal.

Since 1923, Rear Admiral William E. Moffett, chief of the Bureau of Aeronautics (BURAERO), had been looking for a way to stave off Mitchell's attack. Admiral Moffett had to convince the public that naval aviation had certain special requirements that could only be met if the aircraft and aircrews were an integral

From 1919 until 1925, General William "Billy" Mitchell attacked the Navy's role in coast defense as obsolete. But Mitchell was not after the fleet, represented here by the USS *Idaho*. He wanted to incorporate the fleet's air arm into a national air force. U.S. Navy photo.

part of the fleet. By 1924 the job had become an uphill battle. What the Navy needed was a spectacular aviation accomplishment. In April 1924, following six months of in-house politicking, a plan to make a west coast-Hawaii flight was selected as being suitably spectacular.[2] The only problem was that the Navy did not have an airplane that could fly that far.

At the time, the Naval Aircraft Factory (NAF) in Philadelphia had a slightly improved version of the venerable F–5L, which was called the PN7. But the PN7 could barely make a nonstop flight from San Diego to San Francisco, much less a nonstop flight to Hawaii. Still, BURAERO hoped that the type could be quickly developed into a long-range flying boat.

In June 1924, while Army fliers were hammering out Mitchell's air power thesis in a dramatic globe-circling flight, NAF was directed to build two examples of an improved PN7. These two airplanes, designated PN8's, differed little from the PN7's except that they featured hulls of duralumin. Understandably, there were people in BURAERO who doubted that NAF could develop the PN series into the world's longest-range flying boat

The *PN9–1*'s disappearance on 1 September 1925 was the first of three events that brought the independent air force issue to a head and blocked General Mitchell's attempt to absorb the Navy's air arm into a single national air force. National Archives photo 80–G–450705.

in so short a time, if at all. Not taking any chances, BURAERO arranged to have a third transpacific flyer built by Boeing.

Significantly, the Army's global flight ended on 23 September 1924, the same day that BURAERO signed a contract with the Boeing Company in Seattle, Washington, for a long-range flying boat. The contract specified that the plane, designated PB–1, was to be completed in the phenomenally short time of 240 days.[3] (Under normal conditions Boeing would have had at least a year to eighteen months to produce a flying prototype. Because test flights and corrections would have taken another three to six months, the usual practice would have been to issue a two-year contract.) The Boeing plane was considerably larger than the NAF products and was designed to use more powerful engines. (Technical details for the PN's and PB–1 are described in the Appendix.)

By the close of 1924, BURAERO's plans for a transpacific flight were still hazy. This was in part due to the fact that the three airplanes were still under construction. Also, BURAERO hoped that the flight could be scheduled to coincide with the 1925 Army-Navy Joint Maneuvers in Hawaii, to take place from April through June.

The purpose of the flight was to demonstrate with the maximum publicity possible naval aviation's usefulness to the fleet. What better way to accomplish this and offset Mitchell's claims

The USS *Shenandoah*'s loss on 3 September 1925, while the *PN–1* was still missing, was the second event. National Archives photo 80–MS–1.

General Mitchell's public denunciation of the Navy and War Departments, which was reported in the nation's newspapers on 6 September 1925, was the third event. He had attempted to capitalize on the embarrassment that the combination of the *PN9–1*'s disappearance and the *Shenandoah* disaster had caused the Navy. The statement, not the court martial shown here, welded the three events together. National Archives photo 165–WW–434–1722.

than to complete the flight during the largest fleet maneuvers in the nation's history? But the Chief of Naval Operations (CNO) and the Commander in Chief, U.S. Fleet (CinC), refused to allow the proposed flight to disrupt the maneuvers.

Instead, they suggested that the hop be scheduled in June, after the exercises were over. At that time there would be enough ships available to act as guard vessels along the flight path. BURAERO had no choice but to agree, and the start was set for sometime between 28 August and 2 September 1925.

Slowly the plan became more clearly defined but many details remained undecided, notably the starting place. The two choices were San Diego and San Francisco. There were good arguments in favor of both sites, and it was left to the flight unit commander to make the decision late in July. Regardless of his final determination, the preparations were scheduled to get underway in San Diego on 18 June 1925.

Early in 1925, BURAERO was faced with its first setback. It was told by NAF that the PN8's, powered by Wright engines, could not achieve the needed range. About the same time Boeing announced that the PB–1 could not be finished by the contract date and asked for an extension to 10 July.

There was not much that BURAERO could do about the situation in Seattle and the extension was granted. NAF was told, however, that their airplanes had to be ready by mid-May. By this time only eleven weeks remained before the planes and crews were scheduled to arrive in San Diego. In effect, NAF

The Navy's representative in the confrontations with General Mitchell was Rear Admiral William E. Moffet, chief of the Bureau of Aeronautics. By late 1924 the fight to save naval aviation had become an uphill battle, and Admiral Moffet needed a spectacular aviation success to offset Mitchell's gains. National Archives photo 80–G–458975.

had just six weeks in which to produce the world's longest-range flying boat.

About this time the Packard Company offered a 525 horsepower engine, the 1A–1500, which was similar to the Wright engine but much lighter.[4] The low weight to high horsepower ratio was very attractive and NAF accepted the Packards. The PN8's were reengined and their designation was advanced to PN9.

The flight tests using the Packard engines were very disappointing. Overheating, oil leaks, and excessive fuel consumption caused the NAF manager to inform BURAERO on 20 April, "In view of the Power Plant troubles which have developed, the date which the Bureau was assigned for shipment of these planes cannot be met."[5]

But the date had to be met because public announcements about the flight, and rumors that the Army was going to make a similar attempt in June or July, had put BURAERO in a do-or-die position. The urgency to meet the deadline and go through with the flight caused NAF to rush the delivery of the aircraft

When the planning for the west coast-Hawaii flight was started, the most advanced flying boat in the service was the PN–7. Only two had been built and both were unsuitable for the flight attempt. BURAERO hoped that the type could be quickly developed into an airplane capable of making the trip nonstop. National Archives photo 80–HAN–107–1.

before they had been fully tested. As a result, BURAERO attempted to make up for the PN9's shortcomings by introducing some very unreliable factors into the plans.

On 1–2 May, after several abortive attempts, PN9, A6878, set a world's endurance record of twenty-eight hours and thirty-six minutes. On the surface, that appeared to be a good reason to feel confident about the success of the transpacific flight. That was the story that went out to the public. Actually, the record had fallen an hour and a half short of the thirty-hour goal. That shortfall was the project's Achilles heel.

The distance to Hawaii was about 2,100 nautical miles. Based on an average airspeed of 70 knots, the airplanes would cover the distance in thirty hours—hence the thirty-hour goal for the endurance flight. Even if able to maintain the optimum speed, the ability of the PN9's to reach Hawaii was, at best, marginal. Inasmuch as the endurance flight had fallen eighty-four minutes short of the minimum time requirement, their ability to reach Hawaii in still air was nonexistent.

Something had to be done to increase the PN9's range. An increase in airspeed—accomplished through an increase in engine speed—would increase fuel consumption and thus shorten the range. Decreasing fuel consumption was apparently impossible in the time remaining. The only answer was to increase the ground speed of the planes. This could be achieved through the help of the trade winds, which blew along most of the flight path at 20 to 23 knots.

This idea had surfaced in mid-April, and by mid-May the trade winds had become the critical factor for success in the flight plan.[6] The project planners counted on the trade winds to increase the planes' ground speed to around 80 knots. At that speed, the trip would be made in just over twenty-six hours, leaving about a two-and-a-half hour margin.

At the same time L. M. Woolson, Packard's chief engineer, suggested certain ignition and carburation changes intended to decrease fuel consumption. There was, however, no time to complete and test these modifications before the planes were shipped to San Diego. Nevertheless, BURAERO agreed to Woolson's suggested changes, which were to be made in Detroit while the engines were being overhauled.[7]

The result was that the engines shipped to San Diego were not the same as those that had been used to establish the PN9's endurance figure. The endurance figure, therefore, was no longer valid, and the boost offered by the trade winds became even more critical.

By early June, the aircraft had been disassembled and were headed west aboard the SS *Lewis Luckenback*, while the engines were returned to the factory for overhaul. In the meantime the aircrews for the three aircraft had been selected and were steaming east toward San Diego aboard the USS *Wright*.

By mid-June the airplanes, men, and engines were converging on San Diego. There was no doubt about the quality and fitness of the aircrews. The same could not be said about the airplanes. Political necessity had dictated that the usual, time-consuming development process be cast aside. The aircraft en route to San Diego were shot through with deficiencies and

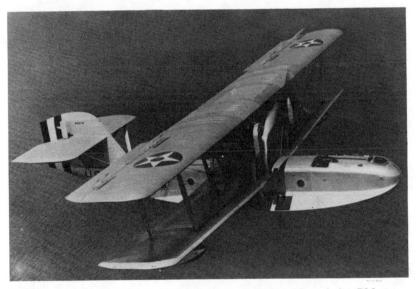

By April 1925 the Naval Aircraft Factory had produced the PN-9. On 1–2 May 1925 the plane fell short of achieving a thirty-hour endurance flight by an hour and a half. Because of the planes' numerous deficiencies, the trade winds became the factor necessary for success. U.S. Naval Institute photo 91731.

were, at best, only marginally capable of making the flight. The plan admitted to this state of affairs and depended largely upon the fickle trade winds for success. The difference between success and failure was very thin. There was no margin for error.

I

San Diego
18 June–22 August 1925

Standing on the USS *Wright*'s bridge when she docked in San Diego on 18 June was Commander John Rodgers. He was looking forward with pleasure to the coming ten weeks, during which he would lead and direct the preparations for the flight to Hawaii. The description he had heard of the PN9's as the most highly developed aircraft of their type yet produced had increased his satisfaction and confidence. Rodgers was in for a big surprise.

The reports he received from NAF and BURAERO were shocking. The PN9's suffered so many engine and structural deficiencies that the list filled fourteen pages.[1] The critical importance of the trade winds to the project further disturbed Rodgers, who believed that the reliability of the trade winds was as doubtful as was the PN9's capability of making the flight unaided.

Getting to Hawaii was a problem he would face later. His first job was to use the next ten weeks to the best advantage and to overcome at least some of the aircrafts' deficiencies. But now he learned of a major stumbling block. According to NAF, the spare parts for the PN9's were not scheduled to be completed and shipped until October or November. Within twenty-four hours of his arrival, Rodgers knew that the next ten weeks would be tough.

From the moment he arrived in San Diego, John Rodgers became the heart and soul of the flight attempt. The urgency BURAERO felt about the project was shared by Rodgers, but for different reasons. There is evidence to indicate that Commander Rodgers lived in the shadow of his famous ancestors, a situation of which he was constantly reminded by his name. The impressive list featured such American heros as Commodore John Rodgers, Captain Oliver Hazard Perry, and Commodore Matthew Calbraith Perry. Not uncommonly, his ancestors' exploits were described by the press while his own record of accomplishments was ignored. In effect, Rodgers was represented as a man who had a tough act to follow and had not yet made his mark.[2] To a certain degree that was true. But did Rodgers live so deeply in the shadow of his famous forebearers that he felt compelled to accomplish something great? There is evidence, though circumstantial, that he did.

Rodgers's assignments during the eight years following his graduation from the Naval Academy in 1903 had been conventional, unmarked by any exceptional event. But in 1911 opportunity knocked and Rodgers hastened to open the door. The Wright brothers had made an offer to train one pilot for the Navy and Rodgers got the assignment. On 17 March 1911, Lieutenant John Rodgers reported to the Wright Company in Dayton, Ohio, for instruction in flying. He was the second Navy officer to be trained as a pilot and the first to take instruction from the Wrights.[3]

Almost immediately after he had completed flight training, Rodgers organized and commanded the first naval aviation detachment at Annapolis. When in the same year he made a series of hops along a Washington, D.C.-Annapolis-Baltimore-Havre de Grace-Annapolis route, he became the first Navy officer to have made a cross-country flight. But most of his aviation activities consisted of administrative matters and experiments with early airborne wireless.

The recognition that Rodgers's pioneer role in aviation should have brought him never fully materialized. Although he was in a field in which the opportunities for success and fame were almost without precedence, Rodgers's accomplishments lacked the drama and excitement that captured peoples' imagination. Rodgers had been designated naval aviator number two, and he seemed destined to occupy a second place position.

Commander John Rodgers was ideally suited for assignment as flight unit commander. He was a natural leader, quick witted, physically strong, and one of the best navigators in the Navy. National Archives photo 80–G–1014484.

Compounding Rodgers's problem and also establishing a more immediate example for him to live up to was his flamboyant cousin, Calbraith Perry Rodgers. Cal Rodgers's aviation career lasted just nine months, June 1911 to April 1912. But in that brief time he achieved lasting fame as the first man to have flown across the United States, from New York to California. His success overshadowed John Rodgers's less dramatic accomplishments, and his tragic death in April 1912 effectively cut short John's aviation career.

The month following Cal's death, John left naval aviation and returned to general service at the suggestion of the chief of the Bureau of Navigation. Cal's death in April 1912 had caused John's mother to express concern for her son's safety, and the Navy was equally reluctant to continue exposing the last John Rodgers to the hazards of flying. For a decade, his superiors and his mother were relieved that John was safe from aviation's awful perils—John Rodgers was assigned to submarines.[4]

Because of his exceptional administrative skills and leadership qualities, Rodgers was returned to naval aviation in July 1922 but not as an active flyer. He took command of, and commissioned, NAS Ford Island. In May 1925 he took command of the USS *Wright*, the flagship of the Commander, Aircraft Squadrons, Scouting Fleet, Captain H.E. Yarnell. When Rodgers came aboard, Yarnell had already received instructions to select the crews for the PN9's, and he offered Rodgers command of the flight unit.

Rodgers was forty-four years old. His service record reflected an officer of exceptional quality, whose career to date could only be described as successful. The *Wright* was his sixth sea command and he would certainly succeed Yarnell, and get his fourth stripe, when the captain's duty tour was finished.

But Yarnell's offer was, possibly, the last chance Rodgers would have to try for that which had so often eluded him. Here was an opportunity to be the first man to fly across the Pacific to Hawaii, a feat that would be enhanced in grandeur as the extension of his cousin's accomplishment. If the flight to Hawaii were successful, it would be more than a novel accomplishment. It would be epochal, a demonstration of American naval power and technological world leadership in the field of aviation. Rodgers accepted.

Joining Rodgers from the Scouting Fleet were three lieutenants. The senior lieutenant was thirty-one-year-old Allen P. Snody, a University of Minnesota graduate who had gotten a regular commission after World War I. The fact that he had

Lt. Allen P. Snody, flight unit executive officer and the *PN9–3*'s pilot. National Archives photo 80–G–459745.

survived the drastic postwar cutbacks was proof of his exceptional abilities. Like Rodgers, Snody came from the *Wright*, but unlike the commander, Snody had logged over 1,200 hours in heavy flying boats. That fact, plus command and staff experience, made him an ideal executive officer. Rodgers relied heavily on him during the next two months.

The next lieutenant, and the man who was to be Rodgers's pilot and most confident and strongest supporter, was Byron James Connell. He had graduated from Pennsylvania State College in 1918 as a civil engineer. On the basis of his demonstrated excellence, Connell had earned a regular commission and in 1924 received an MS in aeronautical engineering from MIT. Connell was thirty-one years old and, like Rodgers, had outstanding leadership qualities.

The third lieutenant selected was Arthur L. Gavin, a twenty-eight-year-old F–5L pilot from the *Wright*, and Snody's close friend. Gavin had entered the Navy at the close of World War I from the University of Wisconsin and had logged over 1,000 hours in heavy flying boats.

Captain Stanford A. Moses, project director, had selected the three officers assigned to the PB–1. The men he had chosen appeared in many ways to be better qualified than the officers

Lt. Arthur L. Gavin was the *PN9–3*'s copilot. National Archives photo 80–G–465315.

who had been assigned to the PN9's. Two were Annapolis graduates who had logged several hundred hours in heavy flying boats, and one had already established a sound reputation in BURAERO's Engine Development Section.

Lieutenant Commander James Strong was in some ways very much like Rodgers. Both were Annapolis graduates, both were large, powerfully built men with strong personalities, and both were seeking recognition. Strong was thirty-five years old, though he looked much older. He had graduated from the Academy in 1915, and had entered naval aviation four years later. He had been a squadron commander in the Battle Fleet at the time of his assignment.

Lieutenant Rico Botta had been in Seattle since 9 April doing what he could to hurry construction along. As BURAERO's expert on engines and related matters he had been ordered to Seattle to supervise the installation of the unorthodox tandem engine arrangement used on the PB–1. On paper, however, he was assigned to the Battle Fleet and was eligible to be chosen as a crew member. The Australian-born engineer was thirty-six years old and was the second oldest man assigned to the project.

Lieutenant Ralph Davison had graduated from the Naval Academy one year after Strong but was six years younger. Of the six officers selected, Davison was generally believed to be the most stable and cool headed. Prior to this special assignment, he had been selected to take part in Norwegian Roald Amundsen's flight across the north pole. He was recalled from that assignment, sent to the Battle Fleet, and on 18 June 1925 found himself with the other officers in San Diego.

The enlisted men assigned to the planes arrived in San Diego singly and in pairs during the week of 18–25 June. Within two weeks the crews were formed. Snody and Gavin, who were already good friends, teamed up. Their third pilot was twenty-nine-year-old Noah H. Craven from Pilot Point, Texas, who had gotten his wings in 1923. Of the qualified pilots other than Rodgers, Craven had logged the least time in heavy flying boats. Snody got Charles J. Sutter as his mechanic. The thirty-two-year-old Sutter had been the mechanic aboard the PN9 during

The *PB–1* crew. L to R: Edward D. Thorton, chief radioman; Lieutenant Ralph E. Davison, described by Admiral Moffett as the
"most level headed in the bunch"; Lieutenant Commander James H.
Strong, aircraft commander; Lieutenant Rico Botta, who had been
overseeing construction of the *PB–1* since 9 April 1925; and Leo C.
Sullivan, aviation pilot, who was the *PB–1*'s flight engineer and
backup pilot. Boeing Company photo 1021–B.

the May endurance flight. Snody's radioman was Clarence W.
Allen, a twenty-four-year-old from Birmingham, Alabama, who
was the youngest man in the project.

Rodgers was assisted by Connell, whose humor and per-
sonality matched his own. The pairing of these two men proved
subsequently to be extraordinarily fortunate. Their third pilot
was Kiles R. Pope, who was rated both as a chief aviation pilot
and a chief machinist's mate. Pope had joined the Navy in 1923
and had been qualified as a pilot since 1922. He was thirty years
old, but he looked a lot older. Rodgers's mechanic was twenty-
six-year-old William H. Bowlin. Bowlin could not match Sutter's
competence in Packard engines, but he was the closest thing to
a jack-of-all-trades that could possibly be found. He knew almost
as much about radios as did any radioman. The radioman was

another twenty-six-year-old, Otis G. Stantz. Because he and Bowlin were the same age and both came from Indiana, they quickly became close friends. In fact, the most notable feature about Rodgers's crew was how quickly the five men became a close-knit unit.[5]

Once the program was underway, the pace was grueling. Looking back on those hectic ten weeks Rodgers commented: "We knew we would be very busy all this time in order to get ready, but we did not realize fully how very busy we would be. The whole outfit was working like Trojans both day and night."[6]

Between 18 June and 30 July, Rodgers did everything he could to hurry delivery of the vitally needed spare parts. He

Lt. Byron J. Connell piloted the *PN9–1*. His assignment to Rodgers's flagship was fortunate. National Archives photo 60–G–460568.

deluged NAF and BURAERO with radiograms and telegrams describing the urgent need for the parts, warning that delay could wreck the project. Despite his efforts, the best NAF could do was promise shipment on 13 August; just fifteen days before the earliest scheduled takeoff date.

Intruding on the already cramped schedule was a host of publicity seekers who wanted to capitalize on the flight. The most influential and persistent was San Francisco's Diamond Jubilee Committee. The state of California was preparing to celebrate its seventy-fifth anniversary as a member of the Union. The focal point of the celebration was in San Francisco, and the planned extravaganza, scheduled to last from 5–11 September, was intended to outdo any previous such event.[7]

The San Francisco committee wanted the start of the transpacific flight to coincide with the 5 September opening of the Diamond Jubilee. Naturally, they also wanted the flight to start from San Francisco. From 22 June until nearly the moment of takeoff, the committee campaigned vigorously for their goals. The only measurable result of their efforts was the mountain of additional paper work that Rodgers had to handle.[8]

In Seattle the situation of PB–1 was already critical and growing worse. When Strong arrived at the Boeing plant late in June, the PB–1 was a long way from being finished. The hull had been assembled, but she had no wings or engines and the interior was only partially complete. Like Rodgers, Strong had only about seventy days to get ready, but until the PB–1 was finished about all he could do was fume and wait. As it turned out, he would fume until 5 August—just twenty-three days before takeoff.[9]

Although by early July preparations in San Diego had progressed somewhat, things were not going all that smoothly either. In addition to the spare parts problem, by 20 July Rodgers was faced with the fact that five major pieces of equipment were either substandard or missing. The only solution was for the crews to design and build the equipment themselves or get the needed items outside the normal supply channels. An official Navy account of the project summed up the situation in San Diego with these words, "As is customary with such ventures,

there was a good deal of last minute scramble and some impro-
vision in collecting equipment."[10] The statement, while true,
understated the situation.

At about this time Rodgers decided to assign the nearly
reassembled PN9's so that the crews could start training on their
own planes. Rodgers selected number 6878 which had been used
for the May endurance flight, and Snody got number 6799.
Rodgers's plane became the *PN9–1* and Snody's became the
PN9–3.[11]

By 20 July, the date on which the PN9's were to have been
test flown, the project was already several days behind schedule.
Nevertheless, with some relief, on 21 July Rodgers momentarily
suspended operations in San Diego and flew with his officers
and men to San Francisco to make the final decision on where
the flight would begin. A start from San Francisco would mean
completely relocating all personnel and supplies, as well as rerouting all future supplies. The move would cost time, and time
was becoming increasingly scarce. Nevertheless, Rodgers was
already leaning toward a San Francisco takeoff when he left San
Diego, mainly because of the nearly 200 miles that would be
saved along a San Francisco-Hawaii flight path.

When the PN9 crews stepped off their planes at Crissy
Field on the Presidio of San Francisco, they were met by officials
of the Diamond Jubilee Committee. There to shake hands and
issue personal invitations to a round of luncheons, dinners, and
theater outings were San Francisco's acting Mayor J. Emment
Hayden, Army General Mullally, and a host of Chamber of
Commerce representatives.

What effect the Jubilee Committee's efforts had on Rodgers's decision to start from San Francisco cannot be measured.
Rodgers later said that they affected him "not at all."[12] But
certainly their arguments fell on sympathetic ears. Even before
the two planes had arrived in San Francisco, the press was reporting that "Rodgers is said to be strongly in favor of San
Francisco. . . ."[13] The press was right.

Rodgers's mission was to get a heavily loaded PN9 from the
west coast to Hawaii within the time limit established during
the May endurance test—twenty-eight hours and thirty-six min-

utes. He had read and studied the report that had been prepared after the endurance flight, and he knew that Woolson had recommended certain ignition modifications intended to improve the fuel economy. But Rodgers also recognized that those modifications were untested and, at best, there was only a possibility that they would work. He shuddered at the thought that the changes might have a reverse effect. On his note pad he put ignition changes in the "if column."[14]

On 2 July Captain Moses had issued "Instructions West Coast-Hawaii Non-Stop Seaplane Flight." In the instructions the average air speed was expected to be 70 knots. If there were no trade winds to help them, and if the time aloft lasted only twenty-eight hours and thirty-six minutes, the PN9's could be expected to run out of fuel at a point 2,023 nautical miles from their start. The minimum distance along the two possible routes was between San Francisco and Kahului, 2,036 nautical miles. But the flight was not supposed to end there since the actual goal was the more distant Honolulu. Clearly, there was a problem. Rodgers added the May endurance figure to his list of if's.

The planners had estimated that the trade winds would blow at 20 to 23 knots along both routes after the 1,000-mile

The *PN9–1* set up and nearly ready to go. The two men in the middle are Schildhauer on the right and Woolson on the left. While Rodgers and his men were in San Francisco, Schildhauer oversaw the completion of both planes and test flew them. Smithsonian Institution photo 79–7182.

point had been reached. Rodgers knew from his own experience while stationed in Hawaii that the winds during that time of year could be variable. The trade winds joined the ignition changes and the endurance figure under the "if" heading. Then he added up the three if's: *if* the PN9's equaled the endurance achieved during the May tests, *if* Woolson's ignition changes worked, and *if* the trade winds blew as hoped. No matter how he arranged them, singly, in pairs, or all together, the sum came out to all or nothing. It was a long way to Hawaii and Rodgers chose the shorter route. The flight would start from San Francisco.[15]

Having completed their survey between meals and other social engagements arranged by the Jubilee Committee, the fliers left San Francisco at noon on 24 July and returned to San Diego. Rodgers had exactly one month in which to complete the preflight preparations. He and many others had serious doubts that the deadline could be met. Those doubts were soon reinforced.

On 23 July, the day before the men returned from San Francisco, the *PN9-3* had been test flown for one hour. The short flight had disclosed a problem that overrode all other problems. The NAF radiators leaked like sieves. In fact, one radiator alone had over 100 leaks.[16]

The situation was so bad on 25 July, the day after Rodgers had returned from San Francisco, that the *San Francisco Chronicle* gloomily headlined, "Hawaii Hop Planes may be Discarded." Several "experts" were quoted, including Secretary of the Navy Wilbur and Senator Hiram Bingham who were then visiting the San Diego Naval Air Station. Bingham was reported to have said that unless the radiators were changed the flight would fail.

Though the headline was exaggerated, the opinion expressed by Senator Bingham was accurate and shared by the PN9 crews. In the words of Lieutenant Gavin, the radiators that had been supplied by the NAF were worthless.[17] The radiators were simply too lightly built and could not withstand the heavy engine vibrations.

The situation immediately became a crisis. Rodgers wired BURAERO that four replacement radiators were needed urgently. In reply, he was told that two replacement radiators were among the spares due for shipment on 13 August and no more were available—too little, too late.[18]

In the meantime, Rodgers had contacted the Douglas Company which had supplied the Army with the aircraft used in the 1924 global flight. Could Douglas supply four radiators of the type used during that flight? Douglas replied that arrangements could be made to have four radiators built by the Flexo Radiator Company in Los Angeles. Delivery could be made about two weeks after the order was placed—around 10 August.

On 28 July, Rodgers sent two telegrams to BURAERO urging approval for local replacement of the faulty NAF radiators. The first message described the arrangements made with Douglas and ended with "Flight may be delayed if dependence placed on NAF radiators delivery." Hard on the heels of the first telegram he sent "urgent; request approval. Radiators most serious obstacle."

The following day Rodgers fired off another telegram to BURAERO. "Request NAF radiators be shipped in advance of other spares. Understand radiators ready." The commander was trying to provide for all possibilities by pressing for delivery by

The *PN9–3*, A6798, on 15 July 1925 in San Diego. Eight days later, on her first test flight her radiators leaked so badly that there were doubts that either PN9 would be able to make the trip to Hawaii. National Archives photo 80–G–4270.

both NAF and Douglas. Rodgers's statement to BURAERO that he understood that the radiators were ready was pure wishful thinking. Maybe he felt that by adopting a positive approach the delivery would be hurried along. Whatever the reason for his choice of words, the barrage of telegrams prompted Admiral Moffett to chide Rodgers in a telegram sent 30 July:

> Intelligent cooperation impossible with conflicting and duplicate information submitted in some of your dispatches. Request more careful consideration be given in future. Bureau is doing everything possible to insure success this flight.

In the meantime, authorization had been given to have four radiators built by Flexo in Los Angeles. Thus, with six new radiators already en route or under construction, the problem seemed to have been resolved.

Troubles of another sort, however, were being considered by Captain Moses. On the day that Commander Rodgers returned to San Diego, the USS *Aroostook*'s commanding officer, Captain Van Auken, had submitted to Captain Moses a list of situations that might occur during the flight. Some of the situations later became awful realities. Van Auken first suggested that the three planes might not stay together after takeoff. He also brought up the possibility that the estimated position of an airplane, as determined by a guardship and the airplane, might differ by as much as thirty miles. Captain Moses, however, contended that with proper care the position of a plane or guard vessel should always be known within a very few miles. In the event that there should be a difference of opinion as to position, Moses left it to the flight unit commander to decide whether to rely entirely upon his own navigation or that of the guardship. He also suggested that the flight unit commander could halve the apparent discrepancy. Prophetically, he added that if the two positions did not agree, it would be difficult to know who was wrong, the plane or the guardship.[19]

Moses made two additional observations. He pointed out that an airplane down at sea had to be recovered quickly since the chances for recovery decreased rapidly as time elapsed. He also noted that a searching vessel might completely miss a downed plane, especially if the plane's radio were not functioning. 31 August, and the *PN9–1*'s ordeal, were still thirty-seven days away. But between them, the two men had accurately described the coming events.

The difficulties that had been suggested by Van Auken and Moses were far down on Rodgers's list of serious problems, which was topped by the radiators. His radiator problem was soon compounded by a bleak report from Seattle.

On 5 August the PB–1 made her first test flight. Shortly after takeoff Strong recognized that the plane suffered potentially fatal design flaws in her engine bearers. He also recorded "dynamic overloading in the ailerons and marked fluttering of the leading edge of the stabilizer." Then, without warning, the forward radiator burst, forcing the PB–1 down.[20]

On the ground Strong took stock of the situation. The takeoff from San Francisco was scheduled for less than a month away. The PB–1 had serious structural problems that had to be corrected. Additionally, one radiator had been totally destroyed, the other leaked badly, and the forward engine had been damaged by overheating when the radiator burst. On top of those problems, the oil coolers were inadequate and needed a 100 percent increase in the cooling surface. In short, the PB–1 was a lame duck.

Strong turned to BURAERO for help. He sent a telegram on 7 August requesting two new radiators and a replacement engine. At the same time he asked for, and received, authorization to have replacement oil coolers and radiators made locally. The telegram was passed on to Rodgers for action. Now, not only did the commander have to get radiators for the PN9's but he also had to locate two radiators for the PB–1 and an entire Packard 1A–2500 engine. The radiator problem was resolved by rerouting the two NAF radiators to Seattle. The PN9's were to use the four Flexo-built radiators that were soon to be delivered.[21]

We can appreciate the intense pressure Rodgers felt by 7 August. The earliest takeoff date from San Francisco was just three weeks away. The movement from San Diego to San Francisco was scheduled to be made in just fifteen days—22 August. The urgent need for the spare parts was undiminished and their estimated arrival—15 August to 20 August—was perilously close to the scheduled move to San Francisco. If the shipment arrived late, the PN9's would have to go on to San Francisco without the spare parts. Too long a delay would push the takeoff date into September and seriously jeopardize the project.

In the meantime, the four radiators arrived from the Flexo Company bringing with them a new, unexpected problem—the radiators were too thick. The additional thickness prevented the installation of the radiator shutters. Without the shutters, the PN9 mechanics believed that the engines would run too cool and adversely affect the planes' fuel consumption.

Obviously the radiators could not be reduced in thickness, and there was not enough time left to have four thinner radiators built. The only solution was to adapt the radiator shutters to the thicker radiators. This meant that still another project had to be completed before the fast-approaching 22 August deadline.

Although concern about radiator failure did not entirely vanish with the arrival and installation of the new radiators, Rodgers's worries were, nevertheless, considerably diminished. The new radiators appeared to be holding together, though the PN9–1 did develop a small leak during a test flight.

In Seattle, Strong, his crew, and Boeing engineers were doing their best to get the PB–1 patched up and ready for the flight to San Francisco. But before that flight could be made the PB–1 had to pass her trials and be accepted by BURAERO. Since her disastrous test flight on 5 August, the big flying boat had been grounded while modifications were made to correct her deficiencies. Though most of the problems were solved, a tractor engine was still needed. In addition, there were still deficiencies in the under-strength engine mounts.

Despite her engine problems and related structural shortcomings, the PB–1 was given her acceptance trials on 20 August. Commander Strong said, "The trial board commenced the test flights, expediting their completion in view of the necessity for reaching San Francisco before the scheduled start of the transpacific flight." Unfavorable weather, poor takeoff conditions, and "the urgent necessity for an early completion of the trials . . . rendered it necessary for the trial board to recommend acceptance of the plane without complete knowledge as to its performance."[22]

Boeing's unique half-wood, half-metal *PB–1* was the world's largest flying boat when she first flew in 1925. Her engine problems were even more severe than those suffered by the PN9's. Boeing Company photo.

On 21 August the Boeing plane was accepted by the Navy and designated the *PB1*. Captain Moses directed Lieutenant Commander Strong to fly directly to San Francisco as soon as the *PB1* was ready to make the flight. A replacement engine and other spare parts had already been sent there, rather than to Seattle.

On the same day Rodgers reported his planes and crew ready to make the move to San Francisco. The takeoff was set for the following morning at 0600. But Rodgers's optimism was short-lived and the schedule was not kept—the *PN9–1* had a leaky radiator.[23]

II

San Francisco
22–31 August 1925

Concerns for success aroused by the uncertainties of the Packard engines had grown into full-blown doubts with the persistent radiator problems. This skepticism grew stronger when the *PN9–1*'s departure for San Francisco was delayed by the last-minute report of a leaky radiator. By the evening of 23 August, even the most optimistic flight officials qualified their hopes for success with a cautious "if." The reason was clear. During the transfer to San Francisco, two of the three planes suffered engine failure and were forced down an hour after takeoff.

The *PB1* was a patched-up cripple when she left Seattle on the morning of 22 August. An hour later, to no one's surprise, she was down on Neah Bay, near Cape Flattery, covered with oil spewed from a ruptured oil line. The cause was the structural weakness of her engine mounts which allowed the big Packard 1A–2500's to nearly shake the plane apart.[1]

After several hours, she again got underway, but bad weather and approaching darkness forced her to land at Coos Bay, Oregon. The following day, 23 August, she completed her trip to San Francisco, arriving at 1300.

While the *PB1* was making the third takeoff of what was to have been a nonstop flight, the *PN9–1* was leaving San Diego with the *PN9–3*. An hour later an oil line parted in the *PN9–1*'s starboard engine and down she went. The *PN9–3* churned on toward San Francisco alone, arriving there two hours behind the *PB1*. She was the only plane to have made the trip without incident. Three hours later, an oil splotched *PN9–1* made her belated landing off Alcatraz Island.

29

The move to San Francisco, during which two out of three planes were forced down, did not tend to bolster the fliers' confidence in the success of the project. The weeks of preparation in San Diego had been characterized by a mood of almost frantic urgency. Although some of that feeling was still present during the eight days in San Francisco, it was largely replaced by a sense of nagging doubt, intensified by the knowledge that the project's success depended on several uncertain factors.

Certainly, Strong and his crew experienced a feeling of pressing urgency during this period because of the fact that the *PB1* was still a lame duck, while the PN9's, by comparison, were nearly ready to go.

There is evidence that from the outset of the final pre-flight preparations, the belief began to grow that the *PB1* would be left behind. With the continuing setbacks of the Boeing plane, any sense of urgency the others felt about getting the *PB1* ready

The first PN9 to fly in San Diego was the *PN9–3*, shown here on her test flight. This flight revealed that the plane's radiators leaked like sieves, a problem that set aside all previous troubles and seriously jeopardized the flight project. National Archives photo 80–G–450705.

in time dwindled. Consequently, the two PN9's increasingly assumed the role of the airplanes most likely to succeed in the attempt to reach Hawaii. At least they were the two most likely to be ready in time. The result was that Moffett, Moses, and particularly Rodgers became more concerned about the minor details that affected the PN9's, than about the enormous structural and engine deficiencies that plagued the *PB1*.

During their seven nights ashore in San Francisco, the crews were quartered in the Olympic Club. The club was also the scene of several meetings at which many major decisions concerning the project were made. The first of those meetings, limited to Moses, Rodgers, and Strong, was held shortly after the men had settled in at the club.

The three men met to discuss the problems that plagued the *PB1*. The major problem, Strong said, was that despite the corrective work done on the plane in Seattle, the whole system for mounting the engines was still too weak. The result was excessive engine vibration which was particularly damaging to oil and water fittings. Strong estimated that the repairs, which involved almost a complete rebuild of the engine foundations, would take eleven days. The flight was scheduled to start on 28 August, just five days away. What Strong was asking for was a six-day delay, putting the start back to 3 September.[2] Six days was too much, but Moses did move the start date back to 31 August.

Strong would have liked more time to complete the necessary major structural changes on the *PB1*, as well as test and tune his new engines. But a three-day extension was better than none. He knew that meeting the deadline, just eight days away, would require almost around-the-clock shifts. Immediately after the meeting he left the Olympic Club and returned to Crissy Field. That night the *PB1* was hauled up on the shore at Crissy Field. Assisted by a special crew of forty-two men and officers, Strong started the enormous task of getting the plane ready.

The following morning, 24 August, the PN9's were hauled out at Crissy Field. The inspection and discussion that followed helped dispel the gloom of the night before. Snody's *PN9–3* had shown that the PN9's could fly relatively long distances without

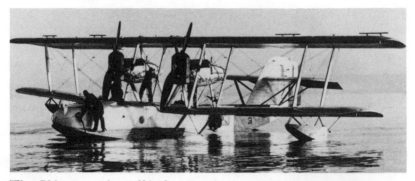

The *PN9–3* topping off before starting out on her nonstop flight to
San Francisco from San Diego. The trip north caused Rodgers to
have second thoughts about his choice of aircraft. The *PN9–3* made
the hop without incident. The *PN9–1* was forced down one hour
after takeoff. National Archives photo 80–G–1032757.

difficulty. No radiator leaks were found and the Packard engines
had, with the exception of the *PN9–1*'s broken oil line, performed
well. The oil line incident was attributed to bad luck. Most
encouraging was the fact that the PN9's were not plagued with
the *PB1*'s structural problems.

Others besides the crew were sizing up the planes. Bets
were already being made on which plane would reach Hawaii
first, and the odds-makers unhesitatingly described the *PB1* as
a bad bet. Still, if Strong could get his giant metal and wood
boat into the air, he stood a chance of getting to Hawaii first.

Snody and his crew were generally touted as the best bet
to finish first simply because the *PN9–3* had been the only one
of the three planes to make the trip to San Francisco without
mishap. Four days later, the odds in favor of the *PN9–3* being
first across the line were increased.

Rodgers, in the *PN9–1*, fit neatly into second place by a few
odds because his plane had already set the endurance record in
May. The odds-makers considered his forced landing on 23 August, but also allowed points for the fact that the name John
Rodgers was a household word in the Navy. The result was that
the *PN9–1* and *PN9–3* were rated very close, while the *PB1* was
a dark horse.

The *PN9–3* was the second plane to land on San Francisco Bay. Her flight north had been made without incident and the odds-makers picked Snody's plane as the favorite in the "race" to Hawaii. National Archives photo 80–G–4293.

By now a truckload of equipment and material, plus sixty metal workers from Mare Island Naval Yard, had arrived at Crissy Field. The extensive work that had to be done on the *PB1* necessitated shifts around the clock. No effort was spared to get her completed, but already the public announcements about the *PB1* were suggesting that she might not be ready.

The reinforcements for the *PB1* had arrived on Wednesday. On Thursday the PN9's were ready to fly, and Friday, 28 August, was set for their test flights. But Rodgers was still worried about the radiators, even though the Douglas radiators on the *PN9–3* and the improved NAF radiators on the *PN9–1* seemed to be holding up well. He could not forget that the transfer to San Francisco had been held up for twenty-four hours when the so-called "improved" NAF radiators developed leaks. In an effort to prevent a repeat of the problem, Rodgers had a radiator sealant known as "Liquid-X" added to the radiator water.[3] The precaution nearly killed him and his crew a week later.

On Friday morning, 28 August, the *PN9–3* increased her lead as the plane most likely to complete the flight. While the two seaplanes were warming up for the test flight, a leak in the *PN9–1*'s gravity fuel tank was discovered. The plane was hauled back up on the launching ramp and towed to the service area.

23 August 1925. The *PB–1* won the race to San Francisco after a trouble-filled flight from Seattle. She arrived in need of an engine replacement and a complete rebuilding of her engine foundations and supports. National Archives photo 80–G–02916.

While the *PN9–1* sat dripping on the hardstand, the *PN9–3* sped across the water and became the first of the three planes to make a takeoff on San Francisco Bay.[4]

The *PN9–1*'s fuel tank was quickly removed and repaired that same day. That afternoon she also made a trial flight over the bay. The sight and sound of the two PN9's getting into the air was particularly hard on Strong's crew. Their airplane was still partially dismantled, the engines were supported by jacks, and many of the newly designed replacement parts had yet to be built. There were only three days left and the *PB1* was falling even further behind.

On 29 August, while being towed by a small tractor, the *PN9–1*'s wing struck a hanger and was lightly damaged. The bookmakers noted another mark against the *PN9–1* as a "hard luck" airplane and gave the *PN9–3* another rating boost for her untarnished record of success. The *PN9–3* was a "lucky plane."

A three-hour test flight that day was a success. The radiators held water, and the oil lines remained firmly connected. After a quick engine inspection at Crissy Field, both planes took off again and flew the fifteen-mile hop to Midshipman Point, on San Pablo Bay. The move to San Pablo Bay, the north arm of

San Francisco Bay, broke the *PN9–3*'s winning streak, but not so badly that the odds favoring her were much reduced, if at all. As she was taking on the full load of fuel for the next day's full-load tests, the USS *Gannet*'s motor sailer slammed into and bent the port wingtip float. An emergency repair crew was rounded up and was sent out to the plane with a spare float. Fortunately the water was calm, and repairs were made without difficulty.[5]

Since the purpose of the move to San Pablo Bay was to conduct full-load takeoff tests, the morning of Sunday, 30 August, was spent taking aboard all the supplies, spare parts, and equipment that the planes were to carry during the transpacific flight. The only supplies not taken aboard were the in-flight meals for the trip.

The takeoff tests were to be made under conditions similar to those expected the following day. Reportedly, the intent at this late date was to establish the maximum fuel load that the planes could lift into the air. During the May endurance test in Philadelphia, a PN9—actually the *PN9–1*—had gotten off the water with 1,320 gallons of fuel, of which 50 gallons were carried in 5-gallon cans. All subsequent planning estimates were based on that figure.

Performing a full-load test on the eve of the flight might seem somewhat belated. In fact, the test should have been done much earlier—for example in San Diego—and should also have been an endurance test. After all, the PN9's now warming up on San Pablo Bay differed measurably from the plane that had made the endurance flight in May.

Because of the untested ignition and carburation changes made after the endurance test in Philadelphia, the performance figure established there could only be an approximation of what might be expected now. Additionally both PN9's would be several hundred pounds heavier than the test plane had been. One more crewman—the May endurance flight was made with just four men—plus additional equipment and extra fuel needed for the transpacific hop had increased the planes' load.

In fairness to the crews and project planners, there had not been an opportunity to conduct the full-load tests until 30 Au-

gust. But the fact that the opportunity came only on the eve of
the main event demonstrated again the urgency with which the
project was rushed forward. In effect, these full-load takeoff tests
were intended to find out if the PN9's could still get off the
water.

A failure on Sunday would have delayed the transpacific
flight but could have been explained to the public without too
much embarrassment. If the tests had not been made and, on
Monday, in full view of thousands of onlookers, the planes were
unable to lift off the water, it would have been a publicity disaster. One had only to think for a second to realize how Mitchell
would have used such an event to his advantage. The full-load
takeoff tests were late, but they were certainly necessary.

At 1500 both planes were warmed up and in position. Instead of a full load, each plane had about 1,260 gallons of fuel
aboard. The extra gasoline, which was stored in 5-gallon cans,
had been left behind on the fuel barge in order to reduce the fire
hazard. To replace the weight of the missing fuel, each plane
took three passengers, described as husky sailors, aboard. The
combined weight of the three sailors may not have been exactly
the same as the weight of the absent fuel, but the difference was
too small to argue over.[6]

Forced landings, engine problems, and leaky radiators had
been enough to dampen anyone's hope for success, and the takeoff tests did not help. The tests were spectacular but showed
that getting a heavily loaded seaplane off the water was extremely
difficult.

Sunday, 30 August, was bright, clear, and very windy. The
entire bay was covered with white caps, heaped up by a 25-knot
wind.[7] Spectators along the shore and hills surrounding the takeoff area watched breathlessly as each plane surged across the
water. Whole walls of water were thrown up as the fast-moving
planes slammed into the advancing rows of jagged chop. The
water, exploding along the sides of the hull in a V from beneath
the keel, was sucked back through the spinning propellers and
spewed aft in a dense cloud of white salt spray.

Water poured in through the open cockpits and sloshed in
the bilges. From the outset the pilots were drenched with frigid

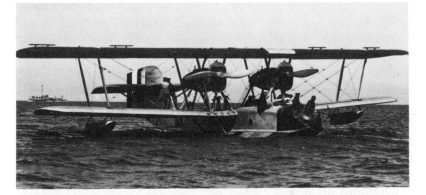

30 August 1925. The *PN9–1* waiting for the full-load takeoff tests to start. There are seven men visible aboard the airplane. The extra crewmen were sailors put aboard as ballast to compensate for the absent fifty gallons of spare fuel. The *PN9–1*'s bow was painted yellow shortly before leaving San Diego. National Archives photo 80–G–4283.

water. Visibility was almost zero through the spray and their salt-coated goggles, and the planes were pounding terribly as they made the long takeoff runs. Only the pilots' heads poked above the hull, everyone else was desperately hanging on below.

Both airplanes made three futile attempts to take off. Neither was able to get up on the step, which would have meant that they were at least close to lifting off. Snody brought the *PN9–3* around for a fourth attempt. But before starting, he off-loaded his three ballast sailors—a practical decision which the sailors wholeheartedly endorsed. With his plane nearly 600 pounds lighter, Snody drove the *PN9–3* through the pounding chop for the fourth time. But this time there was a strange sensation, described as a sharp, rapid vibration, running through the plane as she crashed across the water. One of the propellers was damaged.

Still, Snody kept the engines howling at full power. Then a new feeling coursed through the hull and up the control column. The sound of the plane crossing the water changed. The *PN9–3* was rising up on her step. Snody felt the plane rise, so did Allen, clinging to the frames in the after radio compartment. The *PN9–3* was about to fly.

At this critical moment, when the plane was starting to break the last bond with the water, Snody cut the power. He recognized the unmistakable vibration caused by the damaged propeller and did not want to risk his plane any further. Snody pulled the throttles back, and the *PN9–3* settled quickly and heavily back into the water.

Rodgers had told Connell that they would also try one more time, but the commander chose to keep his human ballast aboard. As the *PN9–3* settled and swung around to taxi back to the fuel barge, the *PN9–1* started her fourth run. This time Connell was successful and the *PN9–1* actually left the water. The plane rose slowly until she was just a few feet above the surface. Those few feet were enough to satisfy Rodgers who signaled Connell to put her back down. Connell simply cut the power and the *PN9–1* made a perfect landing.

The straight run, short flight, and landing had taken the *PN9–1* a considerable distance down the bay. By the time she had taxied back to the fuel barge, Snody and his crew had assessed the damage to their starboard propeller. The consensus

30 August 1925. The *PN9–3* swings around for another try at getting off during the full-load tests. Both planes made several unsuccessful takeoff runs and both were slightly damaged during the tests. National Archives photo 80–G–4269.

of the crew was that the damage was not serious enough to be concerned about. There were spare propellers at Crissy Field, but changing one would mean that the plane would have to be taken there. They may have felt that there was not enough time to make the propeller change. Whatever the reason for the decision, keeping the damaged propeller proved to be unfortunate.

Both planes returned to their anchorage and began taking on the final stores needed for the flight. For in-flight meals, each plane received forty ham sandwiches, twenty-five oranges, twenty quarts of water in one-quart aluminum canteens, and fifty sugar cubes in a one-quart Mason jar. This food was bolstered with two-and-a-half pints of hot soup, and fifteen pints of coffee, in one-quart thermos bottles. Emergency rations consisted of three pounds of hard tack and six pounds of canned corned beef, intended to last three days.[8]

Two unofficial items also came aboard that belonged to Commander Rodgers—a thermos of Poi and a copper still. His friends had given him the Poi, and the gasoline-fired copper still was a gift from his mother. The still was to be used to make water if he were forced down at sea.[9]

Even more important than what was taken along, was what was not. Because of weight limitations, the airplanes were not equipped with an emergency radio transmitter.[10] Considering the nature of the undertaking, the omission of this basic safety device seems curious.

The Navy had a light-weight transmitter, CG1104, which had been part of the equipment aboard the first planes to fly the Atlantic in 1919. The CG1104 was a fifty-watt, vacuum-tube transmitter which could be powered by a wind-driven generator or by dry batteries. In addition to its other uses the CG1104 could be installed aboard large flying boats as an auxiliary transmitter. It had a range of 100 miles and weighed twenty-six pounds.[11]

Since the 1919 transatlantic flight was in many ways similar to the 1925 transpacific flight, something should have been learned from the earlier experience. Just six years earlier, Commander John Towers had removed his CG1104 from the *NC–3* before he left Trepassey Bay, Newfoundland, in order to save weight. Towers went down at sea before reaching the Azores and was unable to transmit because he had no battery-operated radio aboard. Prior to that, on the hop from Rockaway Beach to Halifax, he had also been forced down. On that occasion he had the CG1104 aboard, and within fifty seconds after landing, he had made contact with the USS *Baltimore*. Thus, the usefulness and practicality of the CG1104 had been clearly demonstrated. For a savings of just twenty-six pounds, Rodgers and his crew came very close to dying.

By the time all supplies and fuel had been taken aboard, the PN9's were so overloaded that their wingfloats were nearly awash. Empty, the PN9 weighed 9,100 pounds. Added weight in the form of 1,350 gallons of fuel, 50 gallons of oil, and a mountain of supplies brought the gross takeoff weight to 19,300 pounds.[12] Fuel and oil accounted for nearly all but about one ton of the additional weight.

Their work completed, Rodgers and his men returned to the Olympic Club. During the evening of 30 August, all the officers, including Admiral Moffett and Captain Moses, met to discuss Strong's request for another two-day delay. What followed was one of those unpleasant situations that develops when emotions are high and a decision contrary to the wishes of one of the parties involved must be made.

After dinner the officers met in one of the club's meeting rooms.[13] Despite the informal atmosphere, the meeting quickly assumed the appearance of a hearing. Strong was asked to present his case. He restated his request for a two-day delay so that he would have a chance to be in the "race." Next, he pointed out that for three months he and his men had been doing everything possible to get their plane ready and they were close to their goal. He thought the *PB1* should at least be allowed to start with the PN9's. He was obviously thinking of his career, and appealing to his fellow officers' sense of justice, when he concluded that there might not again be "so good an opportunity" for him "as offered by this flight."

Lieutenant Davison vigorously supported Commander Strong. Acknowledging the risk involved in using the untested *PB1*, he insisted that he would feel personally insulted if he were not allowed to take those risks. Davison believed that the possibility of developing problems was not substantially greater for the *PB1* than for the PN9's.

When Rodgers's turn came, he pointed out that he was not just the flight unit commander but was also a competitor in the flight. He suggested that this might cause "unknown prejudice" in his view. Having already described himself as a competitor, he hastened to say that he did not consider the flight a "sporting event, or in any sense a race."

From this seemingly incompatible position, Rodgers then presented a sound argument for not delaying the flight. His duty was, he felt, to get as many planes safely to Hawaii as possible in order to demonstrate that the feat could be done. He said that the PN9's were ready and "on the crest of their wave" so far as preparations were concerned. They were fully loaded, lying in the water, and the tide would turn at just the right time on Monday.

Any further delay, argued Rodgers, would only detract from the PN9's chances of reaching Honolulu, while giving the *PB1* a doubtful chance. Rodgers's opinion was that two days, or even several days, would not be enough time in which to get the *PB1* ready. He then offered Strong some weak encouragement, and partially supported Davison's view, when he concluded that it was quite possible that neither PN9 would make it to Hawaii. Later Rodgers said, "Time has shown I was a better prophet than I truthfully thought I was."

It was clear from the conversation that despite the official Navy position, and public statements by the officers to the contrary, the flight had become a race in the minds of the participants. It would, however, be unfair to say that Rodgers opposed a delay for selfish reasons. His arguments, particularly in view of the fact that the PN9's were literally at the starting line, were clearly valid. Captain Moses agreed. He told Strong that the decision was particularly hard on him, since he had selected the *PB1*'s crew from among his own command. Admiral Moffett also agreed with Rodgers and said that he "felt keenly" the disappointment of Commander Strong and his crew. The admiral added that holding the *PB1* back was a blow to his pride, since he had authorized the building of the plane without the full concurrence of his advisors. Some hope was offered to Strong that the *PB1* would be allowed to make the flight alone as soon as the Boeing plane was ready.

Rodgers later said that he did not feel good about the outcome of the meeting and was especially distressed over the great disappointment shown by Commander Strong. In a later interview Commander Rodgers made a point of refuting any suggestion that he had deliberately blocked the *PB1* from joining the flight. He described Strong's crew as three of the best officers and two of the best enlisted men in the Navy. He added that had they been allowed to go at that time, they would certainly have met with misfortune. After the meeting both Davison and Strong shook his hand saying that the fight was over and Rodgers had won. "I could not feel that way about it," said Rodgers later, "and hope we parted friends."[14]

III

The Flight
31 August-1 September 1925

31 August 1925 was a bright, fog-free day on San Francisco Bay. By midmorning the water's surface was already rippled by cats paws, indicating that the normal, stronger westerlies would soon follow. Hundreds of small boats and yachts dotted the bay, filled with the lucky few who would have a front-row seat for the takeoff. The beaches and low hills surrounding the bay were jammed with onlookers, and overhead flocks of Army and Navy planes circled. Among the circling planes was the *PB1* which had taken off from Crissy Field on her first flight.[1]

At 1000 a fast powerboat roared away from the waterfront and shot across the bay. From the number of people aboard and the direction the boat was traveling, the onlookers quickly guessed that the PN9 crews were headed toward their planes. Cheers, waving flags, sirens, and horns greeted the speeding boat as it raced through the jubilant fleet of small boats and yachts.

At 1030 the boat throttled back and slid alongside the *PN9–1*. Rodgers, Connell, Pope, Bowlin, and Stantz shook hands all around, wishing their fellow airmen good luck and climbed onto their plane. Ten minutes later Snody, Gavin, Sutter, Craven, and Allen were aboard the *PN9–3*, and the speedboat had gone over to the *Gannet*.

In the airplanes the men quickly stored their gear and began making the last minute preflight checks. Radiomen checked their sets, looked for loose connections, and pressed tubes more tightly into their sockets. The mechanics searched the engines for loose fittings, checked oil and water levels, sniffed for fuel leaks, and hoped the radiators would not leak. The pilots worked their controls, rechecked the stowage of spare parts and equipment, and hoped that they could get their planes off the water on the first try.

During the preflight check, Rodgers found that the *PN9–1* had suffered some damage in the full-load tests but not as much as the *PN9–3*. Salt water, which had poured through the several hull openings, had corroded the aluminum cable that connected the EIC controller on the pilot's instrument panel with the EIC coil. This meant that the pilot could not set the desired course on the controller.

Rodgers decided that the only solution would be to bring the plane onto the correct heading with the aperiodic compass. Then he would set the EIC by hand at the coil, turning the corroded controller fitting until the needle on the pilot's instrument panel was zeroed.[2] The process was cumbersome, but there was no other way.

By 1100 the planes had been cast off from the fuel barge and were taken in tow by two small launches. En route to the takeoff area one of the *Gannet*'s boats came alongside each plane and passed across a hot meal for the crews—the last Rodgers and his crew would have for ten days.

With the planes' gross takeoff weight at 19,300 pounds, just getting off the water was going to be the biggest problem for the pilots. They were counting on the wind and rough surface that the weather bureau had predicted.

Shortly before 1400, the PN9's reached the starting point and cast off their tow. While they were drifting, one of the *Gannet*'s small boats carrying Admiral Moffett, Captain Moses, and several dignitaries again came alongside the *PN9–1*. Two barographs to officially record any distance record that might be set were put aboard.[3] Admiral Moffett also gave Commander Rodgers two letters, one addressed to Admiral McDonald, commandant of the Fourteenth Naval District in Honolulu, and the other addressed to the governor of Hawaii. From his place in the bow Rodgers shook hands with the three men and the boat moved off. The launch next went to the *PN9–3* where two barographs were also put aboard. The admiral's launch then moved from the planes, and the order to start engines was given.

In the abbreviated starting lineup, the *PN9–3* again proved to be the best bet when the order came at 1400 to start engines. Both the *PN9–3*'s Packards belched blue smoke and flame and started without problem. While the *PN9–3* sat waiting with her engines warming, the *PN9–1*'s starboard engine refused to start. The port engine had started easily, but its partner just would not catch. After fifteen minutes the balkey starboard engine coughed, sputtered, hacked, popped a couple of times, and roared to life.

In the meantime, both *PN9–3*'s engines had come up to operating temperature, and Snody had to throttle them down to less than 800 rpm to keep the plugs from fouling. The wait had also revealed disturbingly how badly the starboard propeller was out of balance. The plane was shaking violently, but Snody was not about to quit now.

Despite the weather bureau's optimistic forecast, the strong wind characteristic of San Pablo Bay did not develop that day. Instead, the wind remained light. The conditions for takeoff, smooth water and light wind, were very bad. Snody took the *PN9–3* in close to the western shore where he hoped to gain some advantage from the much shallower water there. Rodgers and Connell planned to start their run into the wind, and then, when the plane was up on the step, they would make a half turn and complete the takeoff along the intended southwesterly route.[4]

While the *PN9–3* waited in close to shore, Connell started his run. For a mile and a half, the *PN9–1*, enveloped in a cloud of spray, strained and bucked but could not get up on the step. The *PN9–1* was well into her takeoff run when Connell noticed the engines were starting to heat up. Alarmed, he cut the power. The *PN9–1* quickly lost way and Connell swung around and headed back for the starting point. The moment Connell aborted the takeoff attempt, the *PN9–3* went to full power and started her run.

Snody took the *PN9–3* straight down the intended run without regard to the light westerly breeze. The damaged starboard propeller set up a pounding vibration that nearly shook the plane apart. Despite the noise and violent shaking, the *PN9–3* continued her long run, slowly rising up on the step as she shot across the water.

Craven gripped the frames behind the pilot's seat, Sutter braced himself amidships, Allen was crouched in the radio cockpit, and Gavin hung on in the copilot's seat. The *PN9–3*, up on the step, but unable to lift off, was rapidly closing on the shore. Snody kicked the rudder over to the left to clear the shoreline and shouted to Craven and Sutter to move back into the tail with as many gas cans as they could carry. He wanted the weight aft to bring the bow up.

As the men scrambled aft, the *PN9–3* continued her thundering charge across the water, riding on her step but refusing

31 August 1925. The *PN9–3*, identified by the yellow stripe around her fuselage, heads out the Golden Gate. Snody was the first away, but his luck soon ran out. Smithsonian Institution photo 74–11671.

to lift off. Suddenly, Snody noted a perceptible change in his plane followed by the unmistakable feel of flight. At 1442 the *PN9–3* became airborne.

While taxiing back to the starting point, Rodgers had all the spare gas cans moved to the tail of the plane and then told Bowlin, Pope, and Stantz to move as far aft as possible. Like Snody, the commander wanted to bring the bow up to help her break loose. Rodgers took the copilot's seat next to Connell.

Connell, furious about his first failure, was anxious to try again. The *PN9–3* was hardly off the water when he rammed the throttles to the firewall. The engine rpm leaped to 2,300 as the heavy seaplane lumbered forward and gained speed. The *PN9–1* plowed across the broken water, her propellers beating up a cloud of spray that hid all but the wingtips and bow. Four miles down her run she was still glued to the surface. Connell hung on grimly, determined to get the *PN9–1* off or sink her trying.[5]

At the six-mile mark the *PN9–1* slowly rose up on the step. Rodgers, thinking she was still bow heavy, left the copilot's seat and scrambled aft. Just as he reached the engineer's cockpit the plane began to lift. With blue-hot exhaust streaming from her roaring engines and her hull shaking until it seemed nearly to come apart, the *PN9–1* broke her bond with the water and staggered into the air. The time was 1455; the flight to Hawaii had started.

Once off the water and clear of San Pablo Bay, the airplanes made a gradual right turn and passed between Alcatraz Island and the San Francisco waterfront. As they flew across the bay the planes were still very low and climbing slowly. Ahead of them was the narrow opening of the Golden Gate and beyond was the open sea. The *PN9–3* went throught the Gate still only 100 feet above the water.[6] The *PN9–1* did better at 200 feet. Connell was so happy to be off the water and flying that he was sure the Packards were humming, "Honolulu all's well."[7]

The air outside the Golden Gate was smooth, and there was no fog. The predicted headwinds were present, but were so light that they had almost no effect on the plane. The light wind at this point was a blessing. But there would have to be

31 August 1925. The *PN9–1* outward bound, approaching the Golden Gate. Rodgers is in the bow. National Archives photo 80–G–460494.

considerable increase in tailwind as they worked southward if the PN9's were going to reach Hawaii without stopping.

The PN9's were headed down the flight path on a mercator course of 240 degrees, true. The line ran from San Francisco to Kahului, Maui, at which point the flight officially ended. The planes would not land at Kahului, however, but were to turn and fly to Honolulu.[8] Stationed along the flight path at 200-mile intervals were ten guard vessels.

Most of the ships guarding the route were destroyers, but included among them were the aircraft carrier, USS *Langley*, and the seaplane tender, USS *Aroostook*. The latter had taken part in the 1919 transatlantic flight. Each ship was assigned a station identified by a letter of the alphabet, beginning with "N" and ending with "W." The *Langley* was just past the halfway mark on station "S" and the *Aroostook* occupied station "V." At the western end of the flight path were submarines and small ships stationed around the islands, ready in case they were needed to assist in a search.[9]

The guardships were to take frequent radio bearings on the airplanes and were to radio information about the planes' position to the ships stationed west of them. When both planes passed a station, that guardship was to follow them down the flight path at high speed for two hours. This was intended to make any necessary rescue quick and easy.

By 1515, twenty minutes after takeoff, the *PN9–1* was over the Farallone Islands, twenty-three miles west of the Golden Gate. The seaplane had just barely been able to climb to 300 feet, the minimum altitude at which Stantz could drop the radio antenna. At 1545, Stantz got his first radio bearing from San Francisco and heard the *PN9–3* working to obtain one also. He noted that the other plane was transmitting on schedule. Next Stantz made contact with the first guardship, the USS *William Jones*, on station "N." At 1704 a radio bearing from the *William Jones* showed the *PN9–1* to be just north of the flight path.

Between 1545 and 1704 the scheduled transmissions and radio bearings were taken according to plan. Around 1720, Stantz noticed that the *PN9–3* was no longer keeping the radio schedule, and he asked if the *William Jones* had any word of the other plane. Unknown to Stantz, the *PN9–3*'s wind-driven radio generator had burned out shortly after the first radio contact had been made. The *PN9–3* could not transmit.[10]

A lookout aboard the *William Jones* spotted the *PN9–3* at 1740, followed three minutes later by the *PN9–1*. Rodgers was gaining rapidly on Snody and came abeam of the *William Jones* at 1758, just one minute behind the *PN9–3*. The flagship *PN9–1* was reported having passed to the north of the *William Jones* and Snody to the south, both within five miles of the flight path. By 1816 both planes were out of sight.[11]

Both planes started to show signs of serious problems when they were only a few hours into the flight. The *PN9–3*'s damaged propeller was causing heavy vibrations which could not be eliminated even by greatly reducing the rpm. Obviously there was a limit to how far back Snody could cut the rpm and still stay in the air. The *PN9–1*'s port engine was operating very inefficiently and required a disproportionate amount of throttle to keep it running at the same rpm as its companion. Both problems increased fuel consumption, which, combined with light winds, was to prove to be fatal. The *PN9–1* was additionally handicapped, having used forty or fifty gallons of fuel during the two takeoff attempts.[12]

Darkness came on rapidly after the two seaplanes passed the *William Jones*. The winds remained light and were gradually drawing aft, but they were still not developing as expected.

Just before dark, Snody noticed fracto-cumulus clouds at about 1,500 feet. The clouds suggested to him that the wind aloft was stronger than where they were flying, near the surface. Snody sent a note to Gavin, who was flying the plane, to begin a gradual ascent with the intent of getting over the clouds. In addition to reaching stronger winds, he hoped the clear air at the higher altitude would "prevent wasting mileage by dodging the numerous rain squalls which were then giving promise of forming."[13]

The *PN9–3* started a long, gradual climb. Five miles north of them, flying very close to the water, Snody saw the *PN9–1*. He watched the tiny speck that was the flagship disappear into the darkening gloom as dusk turned to night. Snody dropped down inside the bow and stretched out on the cold metal floor.

At 1900, when the *PN9–3* was about halfway between the first two guardships, Sutter went out on the wing to make a regular engine check. Gripping an engine brace just a few feet behind the spinning propeller, he probed inside the roaring engine with his flashlight beam. He saw oil. He moved the flashlight beam around and tried to trace the path of the oil back to its source. Though he hunted for several minutes, Sutter could not find the leak.

The mechanic crawled back to the hull and went forward to the navigator's cockpit. He woke Snody and told him about the leak. Sutter did not feel that the situation was serious because the leak appeared to be small, and he was confident that their oil reserve would be able to make up any loss. Snody was relieved to hear his mechanic's reassuring opinion and went back to sleep.

Twenty-five minutes later Snody was reawakened by Sutter shining a flashlight in his face. He woke with a start knowing something was wrong. Sutter pointed to the port engine oil pressure gauge which now read zero and told Snody they would have to land. The lieutenant hurried back to the pilot's seat and took over the controls. Snody did not shut down the oil-starved port engine. He needed power to land and he did not want to

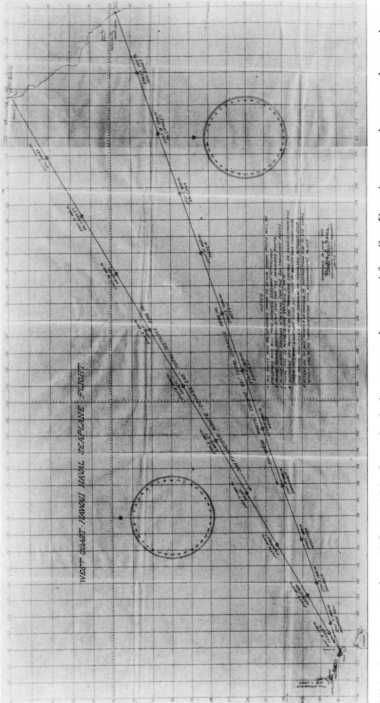

This chart, approved on 19 June 1925, shows both the proposed routes. After San Francisco was chosen as the starting point, the USS *Arizona* was replaced on station "P" by the USS *Corry*. Rodgers Family Papers, Library of Congress.

try an open-sea landing with just one engine. But he knew he had to land quickly or the port engine might explode. In his mind's eye, Snody could already see the smoke and the flame, the huge chunks of engine debris hurled through the midships section like a shotgun blast.

As the seaplane dropped quickly toward the ocean, Snody watched the sea's surface. He did not like what he saw. The seas were high and irregular, making landing conditions extremely hazardous. At half power, Snody banked right 120 degrees, and leveled off twenty-five feet above the heaving surface. Keeping his engines running at 1,000 rpm, he brought the nose up and let the tail slowly settle in. Everyone hung on.

The plane seemed to hover for a moment above the jagged waves. Snody strained to keep the wings level as they lost lift and the tail settled toward the water. The *PN9–3* touched down. There was a momentary sigh of relief at what appeared to be a perfect landing. Then the plane hit a wave.

The *PN9–3* was still moving forward, nose up with her after section in the water when she slammed into the onrushing wave. The noise was indescribable. The *PN9–3* bounced thirty feet back into the air, and Snody rammed the throttles forward in a desperate attempt to keep from dropping one wing. The *PN9–3* staggered, stalled, and crashed back to the surface. Inside the hull men and equipment were torn loose and thrown about with savage violence. Tools exploded from a locker and ricocheted around the hull like shrapnel. Fuel tanks were torn loose and distended by the force of the impact.

Five successive waves pounded the *PN9–3* and the sixth passed completely over the hull before she lost way. The brief terrifying ordeal was over. For a few minutes after the landing there was only the sound of the plane working in the heavy sea. The men slowly picked themselves up and checked on their mates. Snody took a quick count and much to his relief found that there were no casualties. A quick look around, inside and out, was equally reassuring. The *PN9–3* was afloat and apparently intact.

A more thorough inspection convinced them that the aluminum hull had withstood the hard landing and was still sound and watertight. Much to NAF's credit, the *PN9–3* was in no danger of sinking.

The men's satisfaction soon evaporated, however, when they discovered their plane could not take off again. The right pontoon was buckled and bent upward. Several of the previously rectangular gas tanks had been bulged with such force that they were nearly perfect cylinders. The right tail surface support had broken loose at the hull.

Because the plane could not take off again, finding out what had caused the oil leak had become academic. Nevertheless, Sutter dug into the engines and found that the oil feed lines inside both cowlings were broken. The damage had not been caused by the crash. Sutter believed the lines had been broken by the heavy engine vibrations which had resulted from the damaged propeller. He was probably right.

The mechanic was able to repair the broken lines in a fairly short time. When he had them reconnected, the engines were started and used to keep the plane from drifting. The situation was frustrating. The engines, whose failure had forced them to land, were working fine now. But the landing had done so much structural damage that the *PN9–3* could not take off again. Five hours after leaving San Francisco the *PN9–3* was down to stay.

While the *PN9–3* was literally dropping out of the race, the *PN9–1* was hurrying down the flight path. Starting at 2000, for thirty-four minutes Stantz copied radio bearings from the *William Jones* and USS *McCawley*. These bearings all indicated that the plane was slightly north of the flight path. At 2034 the *PN9–1* passed the second guardship, *McCawley*, but was not seen by the ship. The ship's lookouts reported seeing the airplane's flashing light to the north but did not hear the engines. Rodgers said he saw the destroyer's searchlights. The flagship was still very close to the flight path but she was already thirty minutes late. After the *PN9–1* passed the *McCawley*, the light wind began to draw aft, and Rodgers reckoned his drift at a constant 3 degrees.[14]

At 2115 the *PN9–1* made her first radio contact with the *Langley*, still over 700 miles away. During the night, radio contact was maintained with several guardships and shore stations, including a civilian station at Eureka, California.[15] At 2300 the

PN9–1 had begun to receive radio bearings from the *Langley*. According to these Rodgers was still north of the flight path, which agreed with his own reckoning.

While the *PN9–1* pushed on toward Hawaii and made contact with the *Langley*, flight project headquarters in San Francisco was becoming increasingly worried about the *PN9–3*. The plane had last been seen at 1816 when the *William Jones* had reported that both planes had passed station "N." The *PN9–3* had obviously suffered radio trouble shortly after the flight had started. The press knew about the *PN9–3*'s radio problems, and they knew that the last sighting report had been made at 1816. Naturally, the reporters were asking questions about what might be wrong. Admiral Moffett and Captain Moses were asking themselves the same questions.[16]

One fact was certain—the *PN9–3* had gone down somewhere between stations "N" and "O." At 2315, nearly five hours after the last report on the *PN9–3* and two hours and a half after she should have passed the *McCawley*, the *PN9–3* was officially reported missing. The destroyers *William Jones* and *McCawley* were ordered to start searching for the missing plane. Admiral Moffett then called a press conference. Both Moffett and Moses said they were not alarmed and expressed no concern over the safety of the men. Both stated that they expected the two destroyers to quickly find the missing plane.[17] Events proved them right.

When the *William Jones* received the order to start a search for the *PN9–3* she was well west of her station. In obedience to her instructions, she had steamed at full speed after the planes on a course of 240 degrees, true, for two hours. For the last hour she had been leisurely returning to station "N."

The fact that the destroyer was already deployed westward, closer to the forced landing site, helped make the rescue a speedy affair, as did the fact that the *William Jones*'s captain recalled that the flying boat had passed to the south of station "N." Based on observations made when the *PN9–3* flew past the *William Jones*, the destroyer captain extended her estimated track and decided to search along that line. The decision was fortunate. At 2318 the *William Jones* changed course to 233 degrees, true, and proceeded to search.[18]

At 0110 on 1 September the crew of the *PN9–3* saw the *William Jones*'s searchlights and fired flares to attract the ship. Six minutes later a lookout on the destroyer's bridge spotted the flares. By 0200 the *William Jones* was alongside and to leeward of the *PN9–3*. The position of the destroyer to leeward was a tactical error.[19] Before the *PN9–3*'s engines could be started, the plane had drifted down on the *William Jones*. The destroyer's bow sliced into the upper starboard longeron, a principal longitudinal member of the fuselage framing, smashed the right aileron, and bent the tail.

As the destroyer backed away, the *PN9–3*'s engines were started and the plane taxied around the ship's stern to receive a towing line. The keystone comedy continued. The *William Jones* fell off and the destroyer's stern crushed the plane's bow. The situation was rapidly becoming that of the cure being worse than the disease. The *PN9–3* was being more heavily damaged during the rescue than she had been during the landing.

Lieutenant Gavin went aboard the destroyer and took charge of the towing lines. A bridal was passed around the base of the engine struts and made fast to the forward hull cleats, located on each side of the bow. The tow line was made fast aboard the ship and the slack taken up. At 0230 the *William Jones* reported that she had the *PN9–3* in tow and was headed toward San Francisco. Speed was gradually brought up to 10 knots. For the next twenty-nine hours, Lieutenant Gavin looked after the towing lines while the remainder of the crew bounced behind the destroyer.[20]

Twenty-seven minutes after the *William Jones* had started the search for the *PN9–3*, Rodgers's plane passed the USS *Corry* on station "P." Lookouts on the destroyer did not see the plane but apparently Rodgers saw the ship. Radio bearings taken by the *Corry* showed the *PN9–1* to be south of the flight path. This was the first time that Rodgers had drifted south.[21]

While the *PN9–3* was having her run-ins with the *William Jones*, the *PN9–1* passed the 800-mile mark, guarded by the USS *Meyer* on station "Q." At 0220 on 1 September that station reported seeing the airplane pass abeam to the south five miles away. Rodgers's report is in agreement with this.[22]

Bowlin had already expressed his concern to Rodgers about the fuel consumption. The mechanic estimated that the *PN9–1* was using fuel at the rate of about fifty-one gallons per hour—six gallons more per hour than she had used during the May endurance flight. He also told Rodgers that the double takeoff attempt, and the time spent taxiing around on the water, had probably used up enough fuel to cut their flying time nearly an hour.

Rodgers took the notes Bowlin had given him and returned to his navigation table. Clearly, the weather forecast had been wrong. The strong trade winds upon which success depended had not materialized. Fuel consumption was higher than expected and the *PN9–1* was already over an hour behind schedule. Added to these problems was the lost hour of flying time represented by fuel used on takeoff. The prospects for success did not look bright.

Eighty knots was the minimum ground speed required to complete the flight according to schedule—twenty-six hours and nine minutes. Just under 74 knots was the absolute minimum ground speed required to reach Hawaii *if* the *PN9–1* could repeat her May endurance performance of twenty-eight hours and thirty-five minutes. Between San Francisco and station "Q," the *PN9–1*'s average ground speed had been 70 knots. If the trade winds would develop as predicted there was a chance that the *PN9–1* might just squeak in under the wire.

Shortly, Rodgers was made aware of another troublesome find. The exhaust coming from the port engine was a yellowish color instead of being bluish. No matter how Connell adjusted the carburator mixture control, the yellowish color remained unchanged. Bowlin suggested that the color of the exhaust might be related to the excessive fuel consumption and could indicate either carburation or ignition trouble with the port engine. He suspected that the untested smaller carburator jets and the more advanced spark setting had something to do with the problem.

Rodgers agreed but pointed out that the same carburator jets and the more advanced spark setting had been used on the flight from San Diego to San Francisco. On that flight, fuel consumption had been estimated at forty-six gallons per hour.

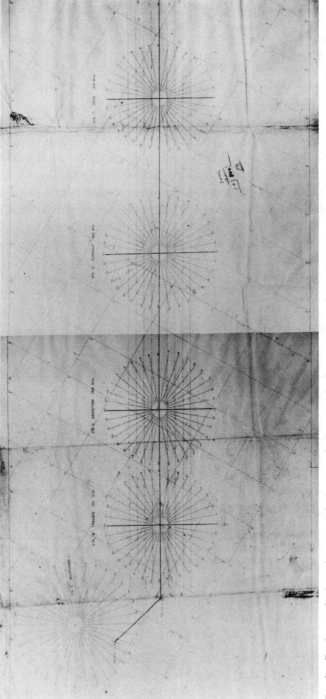

Cmdr. Rodgers designed a special chart and chart table for use aboard the *PN9–1*. A section of the chart is shown here. The chart was 7½ feet long and 18½ inches wide. The course from San Francisco to Maui was laid off in the center and parallel to the long edges of the chart. Therefore the parallels of latitude and the meridians were not parallel to the edges of the chart as is the usual case. The chart board had rollers at each end, and the chart was advanced with a winding knob in the same manner that a roll of film is advanced in a camera. Rodgers Family Papers, Library of Congress.

The commander also noted that only the port engine appeared to be misbehaving.[23]

Rodgers also attributed the higher fuel consumption to increased weight, the need to run the engines at higher than recommended rpm during the first 200 miles, and drag caused by the wind-driven generator mounted on the port wing. Whatever the causes, the problem was certainly real. While Bowlin and Rodgers held their shouted conference, Pope checked the fuel tanks again. He confirmed Bowlin's discomfitting findings.

When the *PN9–1* passed the *Doyen* on station "R," she was still fifty-three minutes late, but she had raised the average ground speed to 71 knots. Radio bearings, taken from the *Langley* prior to the time the *Doyen* was passed, showed that the *PN9–1* was very close to the flight path and just a little north of it. Rodgers, who later said that he saw every ship, reported that he passed the *Doyen* "well to the southward."[24] After passing the *Doyen*, and for the next 400 miles, the *PN9–1*'s ground speed fell off again. The stretch that covered the *Doyen* and *Langley* and ended at the USS *Reno* was covered at an average ground speed of just over 69 knots. The *PN9–1* had been flying at an air speed of less than the planned 70 knots.[25]

They flew all night under overcast skies. Rodgers was pleased at dawn to find the sky cloudy but not fully overcast. There was still very little wind, and when he passed the *Langley* on station "S" at 0730 he estimated that the wind was still just 2 or 3 knots—20 knots less than predicted. Rodgers saw the carrier about ten miles to the southward, but the ship did not see the plane.[26] The *PN9–1* was again north of the flight path.

As the *PN9–1* approached the *Reno* on station "T" 1,400 miles out, the trade winds became westerly and increased to 20 knots—the predicted velocity. The change gave the *PN9–1* a northerly drift of 10 degrees, so that as she flew west she moved even further north of the flight path. This was confirmed when the flying boat flew past the *Reno* and was visually observed to be well northward of the ship.[27]

Subsequent fuel checks showed that the *PN9–1* was not going to repeat her May endurance performance. In fact, the figures showed that she would not even be able to stay in the air for the minimum twenty-six hours and nine minutes required to make the flight. Rodgers had no choice but to land and refuel. The question was where. After the *PN9–1* had passed the *Reno*, Rodgers decided to land at the *Aroostook*, some 400 miles farther west. He could have landed alongside the USS *Farragut* which was between him and the *Aroostook*, just a little over 100 miles away. In compliance with the flight instructions, the *Farragut* had 250 gallons of aviation fuel aboard. Rodgers and Bowlin calculated, however, that they had enough fuel to fly past the *Farragut* and on to the *Aroostook*. Rodgers preferred the latter ship because she was a "fully equipped airplane tender."[28]

Bowlin also estimated that after reaching the *Aroostook* they would have only enough fuel left for an additional forty minutes of flying. The narrow margin did not seem to be a problem at the time. Since passing the *Reno*, the steady 20-knot tail wind had pushed the *PN9–1* along her track at a rate that came very close to the preflight estimate. The run between the *Langley* and *Reno* had taken three hours whereas the *Reno*-to-*Farragut* run took

The USS *Farragut* occupied station "U" at the 1,600-mile point. Her RDF and visual bearings put the *PN9–1* north of the flight path, but her radio transmissions reporting that were apparently ignored. U.S. Naval Institute photo.

only two hours and thirty minutes. At 1252 the *PN9–1* passed fifteen miles northward of the *Farragut*, and everything seemed to be working out as expected. During the next three hours the entire plan fell apart.

Rodgers's dead reckoning (DR) showed him to be north of the flight path with a 10 degree drift to the right. Accordingly, he changed his course 10 degrees to the left to compensate for the drift and bring his plane back on line. His northerly position, relative to the planned flight path, was confirmed by the *Farragut*'s last visual sighting and subsequent radio bearings.[29]

At 1259, the *Aroostook* gave Rodgers a radio bearing of 69 degrees, which would have put him just slightly south of the flight path.[30] The bearing was in error. Considering the 200-mile range at which the bearing had been taken and the normal allowance for error at that range, the 69 degree bearing did not represent a particularly bad error.

More important than the bearing was the additional information that the *Aroostook* was on station.[31] One minute later the *PN9–1* acknowledged the message and added, "still going good. Everything OK." The time was 1300. The *Aroostook*'s position report apparently went unnoticed. At 1314, the *Farragut*, steaming at high speed down the flight path behind the *PN9–1*, reported that the seaplane had passed out of sight. The last visual bearing had been 285 degrees—still north of the flight path.

At 1330, Rodgers received a second bearing from the *Aroostook*. This one also showed him to be south of the flight path. The bearing looked wrong to Rodgers because according to his own DR he was 7 miles north of the line. He was still about 160 miles away from the ship and Rodgers knew that at that range radio bearings were generally unreliable. Despite his doubts, he altered course 10 degrees back to the right, cancelling out the correction to the left he had made earlier. He was still close to the flight path, but now the trade wind would again be shoving him north as he flew west.

At 1357, a third bearing taken by the *Aroostook* was radioed to the flagship. This bearing, like the first two, showed the seaplane to be working south of the flight path. Though the bearing indicated that the *PN9–1* was much farther south of the flight path than had the other two, all three bearings were consistent with one another. Rodgers did not take any action based on the third bearing.

One hour after reporting that everything was going fine, the *PN9–1* called the *Aroostook*, "Running out of gas. Will probably have to land at the *Aroostook* or the *Tanager*. Please stand by." It was a curious message. Rodgers and his engineer already knew that the landing would be made near the *Aroostook*. They also knew that when they arrived there the plane would only have enough fuel left for about forty minutes of flying. They could not reach the USS *Tanager*, on station "W," and they knew it. Why was a message sent suggesting that the plane might try for one more guardship?

The answer may have been that the radioman, Stantz, was already getting nervous. The radio operators on the *Aroostook* later said that as the situation became more serious Stantz's worry became increasingly evident in his messages.

Rodgers had been told that the *Aroostook* was on station "V." Now, at 1416, the *Aroostook* told him that the wind was blowing at her position from the east-northeast, 10 knots on the surface and 15 knots at 2,000 feet. This information on the *Aroostook*'s position and the direction of the wind were vastly more important to Rodgers than were the radio bearings. Together they should have helped him make the right decision when the crucial moment came one hour and twenty-one minutes later. Unfortunately he either had disregarded, or discounted, the *Aroostook*'s position report made at 1259.

Up to now Rodgers had paid little attention to the radio bearings.[32] But the growing disparity between what the *Aroostook* was telling him about his position, and what his own calculations showed, was starting to worry him. Based on everything that had happened so far, Rodgers's logic told him that he had to be north of the flight path. Yet, the radio bearings from the *Aroostook* consistently showed him to be south and moving away from the flight path.

In an effort to resolve the problem, at 1443 Rodgers asked that several bearings be taken. Given enough he might be able to determine if they were right or wrong. In response to his request, the ship took two readings a minute apart. The results differed greatly. The first, taken at 1447, was 38 degrees and the second at 1448 was 158 degrees. Only the 158 degree bearing was sent to the plane. The new bearing was consistent with the three bearings already sent only in that it showed the *PN9–1* south of the base line.

By 1448 the people aboard the plane were getting nervous. While Rodgers fretted over his navigation problem, Stantz sent a situation message, "Getting interesting: just a little gas left in the gravity tank. Out now, wrestling to get as far as [the] *Aroostook*, if possible." The *Farragut* broke in, "We are speeding 27 knots. Following." Three minutes later, the *Aroostook* told the plane to stand by, she would call shortly. Stantz shot back, "Won't be heard. Now have not enough gas to last five minutes longer."[33] Actually, they had about an hour and a half to go.

Seven minutes later the ships were relieved to hear that the five-minute prediction had been a bit premature. The *PN9–1* asked the *Aroostook* for another bearing. The result only added to the confusion. The two bearings, taken at 1500, were terribly erratic. The first one was 198 degrees, followed by "170 degrees or 350 degrees." All three were sent to Rodgers.

At 1503, Rodgers decided to check on the ship's position. He asked, "Are you on designated course? If not, how much off?" The *Aroostook* quickly answered, "Course 60 degrees, speed 14 knots. Heading toward you."[34] Neither the question nor the answer dealt, however, with the ship's position. By his question, Rodgers implied that he equated being on the designated course with being on station. He may have thought that the ship, having started on station, was now traveling on a wrong heading. The flight path was laid out along a mercator course of 240 degrees and passed through every station. The reciprocal of that course was 60 degrees. Therefore, when the *Aroostook* answered Rodgers's question by saying she was on course 60 degrees, she was telling him that she was traveling back up the flight path.

At 1530 Rodgers received a radio bearing from the *Aroostook* of 177 degrees, which put him still farther south of the flight path. Rodgers, who was considered to be one of the Navy's top navigators, could not understand it. Given the easterly wind, his known drift, and his position at 1300, he could not see how the *PN9–1* could possibly be south of the flight path. Assuming that the bearing was wrong, which it was, he held his course.[35]

At 1533 he received a bearing of 181 degrees. Again, his years of experience and training cried out that his DR was right and the *Aroostook*'s bearings were wrong. But the consistently southerly direction of the bearings convinced him that the ship was actually off station and north of him. Exactly why Rodgers chose to believe that the *Aroostook* was north of her station, and to act on the possibility, is not clear. Twice he had been told by the ship that she was either on station or headed up the flight path. He trusted his own navigation and he had already flown 1,600 miles, sighting every station ship along the way. He knew that radio bearings were generally unreliable at ranges beyond thirty to fifty miles, and he suspected the bearings sent to him were wrong.

For whatever reason, he made his decision to use the radio bearing received at 1533. "I was endeavoring to find the ship and not her station position and I changed course to northward,"

The USS *Aroostook* occupied station "V" at the 1,800-mile point. The radio bearings she sent to the *PN9–1* were nearly all wrong. Despite two broadcasts stating she was on station "vice," Rodgers assumed she was actually north of the station and turned away from her. U.S. Naval Institute photo.

Rodgers said later.[36] At 1537 the *PN9–1* banked to the right and came to course 001 degrees. The decision was nearly fatal—the seaplane was flying *away* from the ship.

In the meantime, the *Farragut* was still running at full speed along the flight path. She radioed the *Aroostook* and asked if, under the circumstances, it would not be a good idea to continue on that course after 1500. According to the flight instructions, she was to break off at that time and return to her station. At 1455 the *Aroostook* ordered the *Farragut* to continue and to prepare to search for the plane which was about to land.[37]

At 1500 the *Farragut* broadcast her course and speed and then unsuccessfully attempted to raise the *PN9–1*. At 1520 she took a radio bearing on the plane of 241 degrees, which showed the *PN9–1* to be north of the flight path. This was passed on to the *Aroostook*, and at 1533 another bearing showing the *PN9–1* still flying north of the flight path was also sent to the *Aroostook*. Within minutes of each of these reports, the *Aroostook* was sending bearings to Rodgers which put him south of the line.[38]

At 1550 the *PN9–1* asked the *Aroostook*, "Are you making smoke and flashing lights?" the *Aroostook* answered two minutes later, "Yes." At 1554 Stantz sent, "Guess it would be good night if we have to land in this rough sea with no motors." At 1558 he asked, "Are you in the rain? *Aroostook* is it raining where you are?" The immediate answer: "No." At 1559 Stantz sent, "It is raining here." He then began to send a series of long dashes for the *Aroostook* to take a bearing on.

At 1600 Rodgers received his last bearing from the *Aroostook*, 221 degrees, with the added message "you are very close." Thinking the *Aroostook* must be behind one of the surrounding squalls, he began a search for her in the immediate vicinity.[39] In fact, the *Aroostook* was fifty miles south on station "V"—the bearings she had sent to Rodgers were all wrong.[40]

At 1607, the *PN9–1* acknowledged one of the *Aroostook*'s transmissions, and at 1607 Stantz sent "WEA" which meant, "What is the weather?" The transmission was the last thing heard from the *PN9–1*. Between 1610 and 1614 the *Aroostook* repeatedly called the plane sending, "*Aroostook* on station vice. What is your course and are you trying to find us?" There was no answer.

At 1609 Bowlin was flying the plane, Connell was slumped in the pilot's seat, and Rodgers was in the bow. Pope was crouched next to Stantz, who was just then tapping out "WEA." Suddenly, both engines quit. Bowlin passed the controls to Connell.

Connell took a quick look over the side and ahead to gauge the sea. Then he turned the plane into the wind and started to descend. In the tail, Stantz was frantically sending, "Landing-landing-landing." Pope was trying to get the radioman to reel in the antenna, his pantomimic motions becoming more and more insistent as the plane lost altitude. Stantz shook his head "No," and continued to transmit. He was sending out a position report when the antenna hit the water.[41]

Stantz's last message did not go out. When the engines quit, the wind-driven radio generator stopped too. The little generator, mounted on the wing directly behind the port engine, needed the airblast from the engine propeller to drive it. As the plane glided down, there was not enough wind across the generator's propeller blades to turn the generator fast enough to make power.

As the powerless plane neared the water, Connell brought the nose up a little. The other crewmen braced themselves. Stantz stayed at his radio while Pope, who had wedged himself against a bulkhead, desperately tried to get Stantz to hang on. Rodgers gripped the ring in the navigator's cockpit, and Bowlin, in the copilot's seat, braced himself against the cockpit's padded rim. Connell brought the nose up some more.

Because the PN9's had a high landing speed, experts had often said that the type could not make a successful landing without power.[42] However, despite this opinion and Pope's expectations of a rough landing, Connell set the powerless flying boat down so easily that there was hardly a bump.

The transpacific flight attempt ended at 1615 on 1 September 1925, twenty-five hours and twenty-three minutes after takeoff, and 1,840 nautical miles from San Francisco. The *PN9–1* was down at sea—and nobody knew where.

IV

False Hope
1–3 September 1925

"ALL TRACK LOST OF ONE OF THE SHIPS WING-ING ITS WAY WESTWARD OVER THE SEA."[1] The 1 September banner-headline was not referring to the *PN9–1*. At a time when television was unheard of and radio was still in its infancy, the newspapers kept the nation informed—albeit a day late. On 1 September, while the *PN9–1* pitched and rolled on the open sea, many Americans were just learning that the *PN9–3* had gone down. As far as the American public was concerned, Rodgers and his crew were still on their way to Hawaii.

The Associated Press (AP),using the official Navy time ta-ble, told their readers, "By four o'clock tomorrow, Pacific Coast Time, Commander Rodgers and his men may be expected to come within sound of the wailing ukulele and the cheery bronze Americans. . . ."[2] The estimate was right about one thing—at 1600 the flight was about to end but not within sound of a wailing ukulele. The *PN9–1* was approximately 450 miles from her goal.

Bow to the wind and surrounded by rain squalls, the *PN9–1* pitched and rolled in the heavy swell. In the navigator's cockpit, Rodgers seemed lost in thought, staring sightlessly at the hori-zon, and Connell, utterly exhausted, slumped forward over the controls. Bowlin, sitting next to him, looked around, climbed up on the hull and stretched. Pope continued to brace himself rigidly against the bulkhead until he realized that the plane was intact; then he relaxed. Though the landing had been easy, Stantz had been unseated and was sprawled across the deck at Pope's feet.[3]

Pope prodded Stantz with his toe and told him to get up off the deck. The radio cockpit reeked of gasoline which had been spilled while being transferred from the spare cans to the main tanks. This was the first time Pope had become aware of the strong gasoline fumes, but Stantz was too exhausted to recognize the danger and ignored Pope's prodding.

Pope, unable to stand the gasoline fumes, clambered out of the radio cockpit and stood on the hull. He almost lost his balance and quickly moved to a safer place between the engines. As he gripped the engine struts he saw Rodgers look aft at Bowlin who was now sitting on the hull. Pope was tempted to ask the captain where the *Aroostook* was, but the look on Rodgers's face squelched the question. Obviously if Rodgers knew where the *Aroostook* was they would have gone to her.

Rodgers climbed stiffly out of the navigator's cockpit and crawled aft. Without a word he lay down between the engines and went to sleep. Stantz had finally come up out of the radio cockpit and sat down next to Bowlin when suddenly Connell threw himself back in his seat and said, "I am going to get some sleep." Without another word he pulled himself out of the pilot's seat, lay down on the hull, and was instantly asleep.

The most significant feature of the period immediately after landing, upon which every man later remarked, was the total absence of conversation. Except for Connell's statement about being tired, no one had said a word. The men behaved as though they were in a state of shock, probably due to extreme fatigue and disappointment.

The first men to show any signs of activity were Bowlin and Stantz, who dropped back into the plane in search of something to eat. Bowlin tried one of the ham sandwiches but found it too tough and strongly flavored. He took one bite and threw the rest over the side. Stantz had located the oranges and passed one to Bowlin. The men still had not exchanged a word.

Both men climbed back out on the hull and sat down to eat their oranges. Pope, in the meantime, had located a life preserver and shook Rodgers awake. At the same time he broke the silence. "Captain, here's a little softer pillow than that metal," he said, extending the life jacket. Rodgers took the life jacket and went back to sleep. A few minutes later Pope realized that Rodgers was in danger of sliding off into the sea. He made a line fast to the starboard engine strut, woke Rodgers again, and offered him the line. Rodgers, recognizing the danger, passed the line through his belt and went back to sleep.

Stantz suddenly remembered the kite antenna and suggested that the brightly colored kite might help them be spotted. The idea sounded good to Pope, and with his help the kite was rigged and attached to the light-weight antenna. There was only enough wind to lift the kite up about sixty or seventy feet. Despite the low altitude, the kite was a reassuring sight.

Stantz, who had not been feeling well when he came on deck, now began to feel really ill and decided to go below. The decision was a mistake. He curled up on the floor in the fume-filled radio cockpit hoping to sleep. Pope tried to get him to come back on deck where he would not be affected by the gasoline fumes, but Stantz was already too sick to care.

Pope gave up trying to get Stantz back on deck and returned to his place next to Bowlin. The two men said very little to each other and presently Bowlin dozed off. Pope was now the only man on the plane who was not sleeping. About thirty minutes after Pope sat down next to Bowlin the wind died. Pope looked up just as the kite nosed over and crashed into the sea. To Pope, the abrupt end of the antenna kite was a fitting tribute to the flight.

At 1829, seventy-nine minutes after receiving the last word from the *PN9–1*, the *Aroostook* was steaming at full speed westward along the flight path. Unknown to anyone aboard she was moving away from the downed plane. The *Farragut*, racing to the scene from the east, was directed by the *Aroostook* to keep fifteen miles south of the flight path. The *Tanager*, coming from the west, was ordered to stay on the flight path. Both ships doubled their lookouts.[4]

Several hours later the fliers were starting to wake up and move around. Rodgers inspected the plane and was relieved to find that it had not been damaged during the landing. His main concern was that the choppy sea breaking over the lower wings might damage them. If this were to occur, they would not be able to take off again.

At this point the men were convinced that it was just a matter of time before one of the guardships would find them. They would refuel from the guardship, take off, and continue the flight to Hawaii. While Rodgers looked the hull over, Bowlin examined the engines and radiators. What he found satisfied him that when the fuel arrived, the *PN9–1* would be able to take off and finish the trip.

After inspecting the engines and radiators, Bowlin took inventory of the food and water that was aboard. While he was doing that, Stantz suddenly missed the kite. He asked Pope where it was and was told the kite had crashed. Stantz decided to try hauling in the kite, but a few tugs on the line convinced him that he needed help. He asked Pope to help, and together they hauled in the mangled mass of wood and cloth that had been their antenna kite. The rig was a complete loss. Stantz cut the line away and Pope threw the wrecked kite overboard.

In the meantime, Bowlin reported that the food on hand consisted of twelve sandwiches, ten quarts of water, two quarts of coffee, a thermos of soup, and several oranges. In addition, there was a three-pound box of crackers and a six-pound can of corned beef, which made up the emergency rations. Having made his report, Bowlin decided to have another try at eating a ham sandwich. Again, he took one bite and threw the rest overboard. Connell then decided he would also try eating one of the ham sandwiches. He did better than Bowlin on two counts—he ate half the sandwich and threw the remainder in the bilge.

Stantz was now feeling well enough to join in a conversation which Rodgers and Bowlin were having. The three men took it for granted that they would be found that night or in the morning. The discussion dealt mainly with the refueling operation, takeoff plans, and the flight the following day. Because they were so confident of being found, they gave little thought to conserving their meager supply of food and water. Bowlin's practice of throwing unwanted food over the side was followed by all of them. In addition to throwing away what they did not want, they ate up everything they liked. The oranges, soup, and coffee were nearly gone that evening.

Actually, they had good reason to expect an early rescue. They had sighted every station ship prior to the *Aroostook* and were known to be flying reasonably close to the flight path. The *PN9–3* had been recovered quickly by the *William Jones* at night, and there was no reason to expect that the *PN9–1* would not be found just as quickly.[5]

They also believed that the *PN9–1* could be seen easily on a clear day because of her distinctive shape and color scheme.[6] At night they could show her range light, ignite wing flares, and fire aerial flares. Regardless of all their reasons for optimism, their lack of concern about food and water—especially water—was foolish.

Stantz was soon feeling sick again and dropped out of the conversation. Shortly after the radioman had gone below, Rodgers went forward to the navigator's cockpit to work out their position. What he saw came as a blow. He now knew exactly where he was, and frustration, disappointment, and anger welled inside him as he realized what had happened. Rodgers saw that up to the time he changed course to 001 degrees, his DR navigation had been faultless. As the *PN9–1* pitched and rolled on the empty ocean in the fast fading light, Rodgers saw the awful truth—had he ignored the last radio bearing and stuck to his DR, he would have flown close enough to the *Aroostook* to have seen her.[7] As it was, the *PN9–1* was down at 24 degrees 04 minutes north, 152 degrees 04 minutes west, or about fifty nautical miles north and slightly east of the *Aroostook*'s position.

Connell went forward and joined the commander. Rodgers showed him the position he had worked out and the radio bearings they had been given. Connell thought that the *Aroostook* had given them reciprocal bearings, a common error, but one which was preventable. He based his opinion on the 181 degree bearing, given to them at 1533, the reciprocal of which was 001 degrees. Had the *Aroostook* sent them 001 degrees, the *PN9–1* would have reversed the 001 degree bearing to 181 degrees and flown down it to the ship.

Rodgers told Connell that he had believed the same thing, until he had looked at all the other bearings. He showed Connell that the first two were clearly in error. Rodgers suggested that the next four might have been reversed by the *Aroostook*'s radio operator, because as a group their reverse bearings were a reasonable approximation of the *PN9–1*'s position during those times. The seventh bearing, he said, was wholly mistaken, and the eighth was so far off that it could only be attributed to operator error.

In Rodgers's opinion, the first two bearings had established in the operator's mind that the *PN9–1* was working south of the flight path. Subsequent bearings seemed to confirm that belief and the operator was unaware that he was 180 degrees off on at least four of the bearings. He was apparently confused at 1500 when he sent them a bearing as being "either 187 degrees or 350 degrees." He interpreted a second bearing, taken at the same time, as being 198 degrees and that convinced him that the *PN9–1* was actually south of the base line.[8]

Next, Rodgers and Connell considered the problem of damage by the sea to the lower wings. Both men climbed up on the hull and watched the water breaking over the wings. The sure way to prevent any damage was to remove wing fabric. If the lower wing fabric were removed, however, they would be unable to take off again. Still believing that they would be found quickly, they decided to wait before they removed any fabric.

Night was coming on quickly and Connell turned on the range light atop the upper wing. Rodgers set up a watch schedule, assigning the first watch to himself. A bucket was put out as a sea anchor to slow their drift and keep them on station. The *PN9–1* settled down for the night. Nearly 100 miles south, the *Farragut* and *Aroostook* were searching for them—in the wrong place.

"FAILURE OF FUEL MAY HAVE SENT FIVE AVIATORS TO THEIR DEATH." America awoke on 2 September to read that the attempt to fly to Hawaii non-stop had failed. Readers were assured that the "entire resources of the United States Navy in the Hawaiian district" were concentrated on the search for the airplane. The Associated Press described Navy officials as "expressing every confidence in Commander Rodgers," while admitting their own "anxiety over the predicament of the aviators." The general feeling conveyed by the press matched that of Rodgers and his crew—a problem existed but would shortly be resolved.[9]

As the papers went to press, the *PN9–1* was drifting slowly westward. Stantz woke up at midnight feeling a little better and crawled out on the hull to relieve Rodgers on watch. After telling Stantz to call if he saw anything, Rodgers went below and Stantz was alone. The sea had calmed considerably and the night air was warm. There were large cloud formations but no overcast, and visibility was reasonably good. Suddenly, Stantz thought he saw a searchlight against the clouds and excitedly called Rodgers on deck. Just as Rodgers's head poked out of the forward cockpit, the slowly drifting clouds moved enough to reveal that the "searchlight" was just the moon. Sheepishly Stantz informed Rodgers of his error.

The rest of the night was uneventful, and at dawn on 2 September the sea was fairly smooth, giving the plane an easier motion. The improvement helped overcome some of the men's disappointment and boosted morale. They were talkative and Connell mentioned how easy it would be to get the plane off the water if they only had fuel. Stantz offered the opinion that they would be found right away and Connell agreed enthusiastically. He confidently told how he was going to fly in just as soon as they had fuel. Pope did not want to refuel and go on but to

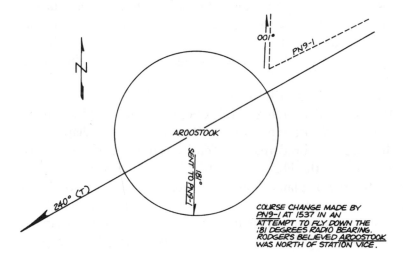

COURSE CHANGE MADE BY *PN9–1* AT 1537 IN AN ATTEMPT TO FLY DOWN THE .81 DEGREES RADIO BEARING. RODGERS BELIEVED *AROOSTOOK* WAS NORTH OF STATION VICE.

refuel and return to San Francisco for another try. Rodgers
assured them that they would make the flight again.

They also talked about what had gone wrong. All agreed
that not getting the expected winds was the main cause of their
failure. Their often repeated expression, "Wind we had every
right to expect," was evidence of their disappointment. They
also agreed that the rain squalls had interfered with their search
for the *Aroostook*, but Stantz had unkind words for the *Aroostook*'s
radio operator. He recounted how during the last hour of flight
the *Aroostook* often delayed five to six minutes before answering
a request for a radio bearing. "Each time I asked for a bearing
she would tell me to wait, and several times after waiting she
would tell me to test again. Finally I asked them what was wrong
but there was no answer." Stantz's listeners agreed that someone
should tell the *Aroostook* what they thought about slow radio
operators.

They were so certain that rescue was just a short time away
that they continued to eat and drink without considering what
would happen if they were not found. Several partially eaten
sandwiches were tossed overboard before Rodgers finally warned
them that they might later need the food. His words were the
first hint that rescue might not be as quick and certain as they
thought, and an uneasy quiet fell over the plane.

At about this time they began to think about using their
radio. But without engines, the transmitter, which was powered
by the wind-driven generator, could not be operated. They
could, however, receive messages if they rigged an antenna and
used a storage battery for power.[10]

While Stantz was working out on the lower wing lashing
the antenna in place, he suddenly became violently ill again.
Connell immediately saw that Stantz was too sick to continue
working and ordered him into the plane. The pilot took the radio
operator's place and went out on the wing to finish rigging the
wire. He was joined by Bowlin. Back inside the airplane Stantz
made the connections at the radio while the others kidded him
about his problem. The good-natured jabs continued until Bowlin looked into the cockpit and saw how sick Stantz really was.
After that the kidding stopped, and Stantz was told to go topside
while Bowlin took his place at the radio.

With an antenna rigged, they began to copy messages from the searching ships. The exceptional strength of the signals made them believe the ships were very close. As a result morale took a big jump, only to be dashed when the position reports showed the search being conducted too far south and west. The *PN9–1* was like a man with a gagged mouth. They could hear people looking for them, but they could not call out.

While the antenna was being rigged, Rodgers took his morning sight. On the previous evening he had estimated their drift rate at about 5 knots, but now he saw that their drift rate was actually only 2 knots. He wondered if the searchers had also overestimated the *PN9–1*'s drift. If they had, that might explain, in part, why the search was being conducted so far south and west. Rodgers felt the first pangs of worry. A combination of an overestimated drift and erroneous bearings might mean the *PN9–1* was in for a long, slow trip to Hawaii. He was right.

Having worked out the morning position, Rodgers went aft and joined the others for breakfast—or what passed for breakfast. He now opened the thermos full of poi given to him by his friends only to discover that the contents had gone bad. Disappointed, he recapped the bottle and tossed the thermos into the bilge. He looked over at Connell, who was contemplating another attack on a now moldy ham sandwich. After thinking about it, Connell decided the awful looking sandwich was more than he could stomach and tossed the ugly mess into the bilge with the thermos. He and Rodgers had water for breakfast.

Back in San Francisco, the *PN9–3* had just cast off her tow and started her engines. Carefully, she powered across the glassy surface of the bay toward the launching ramp at Crissy Field. As several men in bathing suits waded out into the chill water to make lines fast, the engines were shut down and the seaplane drifted toward the beach. Nearly thirty hours after having been taken in tow, Snody and his crew were finally able to climb out of their cramped quarters.

When the *William Jones* dropped her hook off the Presidio of San Francisco, the inspection of the *PN9–3* was already underway. It was soon decided that the damage was more than the shops at Crissy Field could handle. Arrangements were made

2 September 1925. The *PN9–3* back at Crissy Field where the decision was made to tow her to Mare Island for repair. Note the damage on the starboard upper wing. National Archives photo 80–G–4282.

to have the *PN9–3* towed to the Mare Island Navy Shipyard for repair.[11]

At the same moment, nearly 2,000 miles west, the *Aroostook*, *Farragut*, and *Tanager* were starting their first search pattern. Assisted by submarines, they were working a rectangular area which lay between latitude 23 degrees 30 minutes and 22 degrees 15 minutes, at top and bottom, with longitude 53 degrees 35 minutes and 155 degrees forming the sides. The area was based on their estimate of the plane's position when it went down and the assumed drift.[12] Both estimates were wrong.

The *Aroostook* had taken charge of the local searching operations. The submarines were asked to search between 21 degrees 30 minutes and 23 degrees 30 minutes, and as far east as station "V." This meant that the search area allotted to the submarines encompassed the area being worked by the three surface vessels and extended farther eastward. The easternmost limit of the submarines' search area brought the boats roughly on line with the *PN9–1*'s noon position on 2 September.[13] Unfortunately, the old expression that "close only counts in horseshoes" was true here. The upper limit of the submarines' search zone was too far south.

Meanwhile, aboard the *PN9–1*, the crew was feeling the first pangs of boredom. Once the job of rigging the antenna had been finished there was very little for them to do. Stantz and Bowlin traded off monitoring the radio and Rodgers spent some time working out their position. No formal watches were stood during the day. Most of the time was spent sitting atop the upper wing expecting to be rescued any minute despite what they were hearing on the radio. Unless the search shifted more to the north and east, there would be no early rescue. Still, they sat on the wing and waited. Hope died hard.

Later in the day, Stantz copied a message directing the submarines to retire at night to a line along longitude 156 degrees. With the *Aroostook*, *Farragut*, and *Tanager* already too far west, the submarines operating along a line through station "V" had offered the best chance for being rescued. Now that chance was being eliminated. When Stantz told the others what he had heard, their hopes for an early rescue began to fade.

Despite the news about the submarines, morale was still pretty good and, in Connell's words, the crew "enjoyed a much needed rest." At one point, when disappointment seemed about to become a problem, Rodgers joked that people who paid to go yachting often experienced more discomforts than they had on the *PN9–1*.

Rodgers had spoken too soon. The sea, which had been relatively smooth all day, turned rough in the evening. Soon the waves were again breaking over the lower wings, exerting hundreds of pounds of pressure on them. Rodgers and Connell, who still optimistically anticipated resuming their flight to Hawaii, became alarmed. Their worry increased as they saw the rear spar on the lower starboard wing buckle. If the wing folded up, the wing pontoon would fail and the *PN9–1* would roll over. The decision had been made for them; Rodgers ordered the fabric outboard of the struts removed. He hoped that this would still leave the airplane with enough fabric to take off again.

While Rodgers and his crew stripped the fabric from the *PN9–1*'s outer wing ends, Snody and his crew were in San Francisco stripping the *PN9–3* of all equipment and stores. When this was completed, the plane would be towed to Mare Island for repair. The job took most of the day. By 1500, a subchaser was standing off Crissy Field ready to take the *PN9–3* in tow. Craven and Sutter boarded the plane and taxied out to the waiting ship.

The tow went well until the *PN9–3* was nearly to the entrance of the Mare Island Channel. Because the plane was completely stripped of all equipment, most of the weight was forward and the plane did not properly ride the wake of the towing ship. When the tow crossed the wake of a passing ferry the combination of tail wind, strong chop, and the ferry's heavy wake caused the *PN9–3* to yaw violently. One side of the tow bridal parted. The uneven force caused by the broken bridal slewed the plane around. The bow dipped and hundreds of gallons of water poured through the open navigator's cockpit. The *PN9–3* pivoted on her rapidly filling bow, the tail rose, and the right wing tip stabbed into the water. For a moment the *PN9–3* stood on her nose and one wing tip. As the tow line snapped out of the water and went bar taut, the *PN9–3* gave up the unequal struggle and flipped on her back.[14]

When the wing went under and the plane started to roll over, Craven and Sutter bailed out. They were quickly rescued by the subchaser which had cast off the tow when the plane flopped over. Standing on the ship's deck the sodden aviators drew little satisfaction from the fact that the experts were right— the empty gasoline tanks did keep the plane afloat.[15]

3 September 1925. The *PN9–3* starting her tow to Mare Island. A few hours after this photo was taken, the *PN9–3* was swamped and capsized at the entrance to the Mare Island Channel. National Archives photo 80–G–4286.

While the *PN9–3* floated belly up on San Francisco Bay, rough seas were keeping the uncomfortable *PN9–1* crew awake. The sleepless crew sat around and discussed the chances of being rescued. The search vessels' position report disturbed them, and for the first time the men began to worry about not being found.

About this time, Bowlin copied a message from the *Aroostook*. "If you see *Aroostook* near you, fire star shell or show light. We thought we saw a flare ahead." Everyone aboard the *PN9–1* knew that any flare the *Aroostook* might have seen had not come from them. Nevertheless, the signal was so strong they felt she must be very close. Pope fired three evenly spaced flares. The crew searched every mile of the horizon for an answering signal, or some other sign that they had been seen. Nothing happened. After a while the men climbed down off the upper wing and went below.

The flare the *Aroostook* had referred to was later determined to be the planet Venus.[16] On the searching vessels, hope and expectations, which had jumped when the sighting was reported, subsided. No one said so, but the searchers were starting to worry.

While Rodgers and his crew spent an uncomfortable night, a second event, with which they would be forever linked, started to unfold. In Lakehurst, New Jersey, the navy airship USS *Shenandoah* left her mooring mast to start a publicity flight across the midwest. Her captain, Zachary Lansdowne, had objected to the flight because of unfavorable weather conditions along the route. His objections had been overruled, however, and despite his misgivings the *Shenandoah* left as scheduled.[17]

That night while the slowly drifting seaplane pitched and rolled, the crewmen of the *Shenandoah*, several thousand miles away, were fighting to save their ship and their lives. They lost the fight near Byesville, Ohio. Caught in a line squall, the *Shenandoah* was tossed about and finally broke apart. Fourteen of her crew died. On 3 September the connection between the airship disaster and the missing seaplane had not yet been made. The two occurrences, however, were about to be joined in an explosive event that would insure the future of the Navy's air arm. The powder charge was laid and needed only a fuse—General William "Billy" Mitchell would provide one shortly.

On the morning of 3 September, while growing crowds were tearing the *Shenandoah* apart for souvenirs, the men on the *PN9–1* were starting their second full day at sea. At 0800, Bowlin, who had just finished his watch, saw smoke on the horizon. He watched intently for a few minutes and yelled, "Pope, I see smoke! Come up. See what that ship looks like."

The shout woke everyone. They all scrambled up on the hull to see what Bowlin had spotted. He was still yelling, "I see smoke ahead!" as Connell came up on deck. The steamer was already close enough to be recognized as a merchant ship and not one of the searching Navy ships. The freighter was west of them and still not completely over the horizon, but the jubilant men were already discussing how they would have the steamer radio the Navy for fuel. The freighter seemed to be heading right for them. Stantz, Bowlin, and Pope jumped up on the upper wing. Stantz took off his shirt and waved it back and forth over his head. Bowlin grabbed the signal gun and fired flares as fast as he could load, until Rodgers told him to wait for the ship to come nearer.

Connell had gone below and now returned with the plane's only set of binoculars. He and Rodgers watched the freighter and then passed the glasses around. Pope shouted that he could make her out very plainly causing Stantz to redouble his shirt-waving efforts.

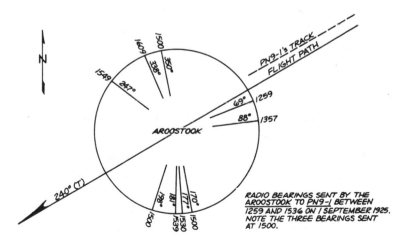

RADIO BEARINGS SENT BY THE AROOSTOOK TO PN9-1 BETWEEN 1259 AND 1536 ON 1 SEPTEMBER 1925. NOTE THE THREE BEARINGS SENT AT 1500.

Stantz suddenly realized that if they had been spotted there might be some important radio traffic going on. He jumped down off the wing and dropped into the radio cockpit. He was quickly replaced on the wing by Connell, who removed a wing flare and ignited it. When the flare burned out he attached a piece of wing fabric to a stick and waved it back and forth. Below, in the radio cockpit, Stantz was trying to transmit by tapping the grid lead of the receiver. Rodgers and Bowlin had moved as far aft as possible and started a fire in a bucket. They used oil and wing fabric for fuel and soon had thick black clouds of smoke boiling skyward.

The freighter steamed tantalizingly along the horizon, not getting any closer. Connell continued to wave the piece of fabric until he was exhausted. Rodgers, Bowlin, and Pope made smoke and Stantz did everything he could to get a message out. At 1000 hours the ship passed out of sight without seeing them.

The men were dumbfounded that they had not been seen. All agreed that the freighter had passed within five miles of them and they had done everything possible to attract her attention. Pope later commented, "We were one sorry looking bunch as we sat there and saw her pass out of sight." Both Rodgers and Connell realized why they had not been seen—the *PN9-1* had been between the freighter and the low-hanging morning sun.[18]

Silently, the men went back to waiting. Bowlin dumped the bucket's hot contents into the sea and threw the bucket into the bilge. Stantz sat at his radio. Rodgers and Connell sat together between the engines and talked about the situation. Pope sprawled on the upper wing and was soon joined by Bowlin. The men were depressed and demoralized by the occurrence. They had not yet given up hope, but as the second day wore on Rodgers and his crew started to worry. Although they still expected to be found, they were afraid that rescue might come too late to allow them to refuel and fly on.

The general opinion of flight project headquarters was similar to that held by Rodgers and his crew on the second day. There was worry, but hope had not died. Nevertheless, Admiral Moffett sent sympathy telegrams to the next of kin.[19]

After the freighter had passed, Stantz picked up the report

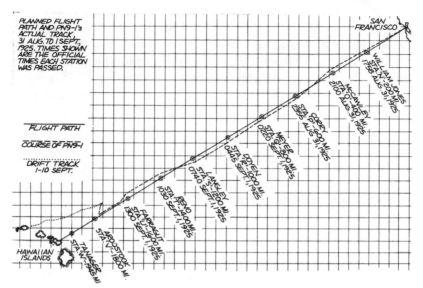

PLANNED FLIGHT PATH AND PN9-1's ACTUAL TRACK, 31 AUG. TO 1 SEPT., 1925. TIMES SHOWN ARE THE OFFICIAL TIMES EACH STATION WAS PASSED.

FLIGHT PATH

COURSE OF PN9-1

DRIFT TRACK 1-10 SEPT.

SAN FRANCISCO

HAWAIIAN ISLANDS

on the *Shenandoah* disaster being radioed through the fleet. He was appalled at what had happened. For a moment he forgot his own predicament as he learned the extent of the tragedy. There was a horrified silence when he told the others what he had heard. They all had had friends aboard her.

The *Shenandoah* crash stunned the nation. The disaster all but pushed news about the *PN9–1* off the front page.[20] Whereas the transpacific attempt was recognized as involving certain dangers, the *Shenandoah* flight had been routine. Her size alone gave her an aura of indestructibility, and her violent destruction seemed as unnatural as it seemed impossible.

The situation looked bad for the Navy. Rodgers and his crew had disappeared just two days earlier while making a flight for which presumably every possible safety measure had been taken. The *Shenandoah* had been torn apart twelve hours after she left on a much publicized routine flight to visit several state fairs. Two major disasters in two days created more bad press than Admiral Moffett and the Navy Department cared to have.

On the afternoon of 3 September, Secretary of the Navy Wilbur announced that any proposed flight to Hawaii by the *PB1* was cancelled. The AP reported that "the practical abandonment of the flight was attributed to belief on the part of the

Secretary and many ranking Naval Officers that the Navy had had enough trouble for a while."[21]

Commander Strong and his crew were unhappy about the secretary's decision. Admiral Moffett, supporting their earnest desire to go ahead with the flight, told the press that he regretted the decision and added:

> Of course I regret these two disasters, but we believe now is the time for the *PB1* to make this flight, while the weather conditions are propitious and the ships guarding the course to Hawaii are in position. The men of the *PB1*'s crew are ready and anxious to make the attempt and to show the country that the Navy is ready to press on.[22]

Strong support and earnest desire could not overcome the fact that the *PB1* was in no shape to make the flight. This fact was dramatically demonstrated a few days later on 6 September. On that date the *PB1* was forced down with a broken oil line after being airborne for just under two hours. On 9 September a second test flight ended five minutes after takeoff when the forward engine overheated causing the engine to seize up.

Nor were all the guardships still in position. Three were searching for the *PN9–1*, and the *William Jones* was anchored in San Francisco Bay, leaving only six ships along the flight path. Weather conditions may have been propitious for the flight, but that was all.

Shortly after Admiral Moffett's statement to the press, Captain Moses made all vessels connected with the flight available for the search. The *Langley*, on station "S" 1,200 miles from San Francisco, immediately started at full speed for station "V," 600 miles away.[23]

By noon the second day, Rodgers and his men began to realize that rescue would not happen right away. In fact, the nagging feeling was developing that there might not be a rescue at all. Connell collected the remaining food and water. He found that they had only seven quarts of water, five sandwiches, and two quarts of cold coffee. The emergency rations, the six-pound can of corned beef called "Canned Willie," and the three-pound box of crackers known as "Hardtack," had not yet been opened.

Connell unwrapped each of the five sandwiches and found

them all moldy. Gingerly he peeled off the ham and carefully scraped the mold from the bread, which he laid out on the upper wing. When asked what he was doing Connell said he was making toast.

After taking a bite of ham, which Connell described as "strong enough to knock you down," he laid the meat out on the wing next to the bread. "I hoped it would improve it," he later said. Each man was given a canteen of water for his own, on which he wrote his name. The remaining two canteens, plus the coffee, were given to Commander Rodgers to be held in reserve.

Their experience with the freighter that morning had convinced them that some sort of battery-powered transmitter was needed. They missed the CG1104 auxiliary transmitter which had not been installed because of the extra weight. The only thing to do now was to jury rig something with the wind-driven generator so that the plane's transmitter could be used. Bowlin suggested that they might be able to drive the generator with the Aeromarine starter and flywheel from one of the engines. The idea sounded good, and they started at once to remove the starter and flywheel from the starboard engine.

The job took all day because the emergency tool kit lacked many of the special tools needed and, to complicate matters, the sea was getting rougher. The metal paneling was removed and the reserve oil tank was pulled out. Several other engine parts also had to be removed to make room for Bowlin to get at the nuts and bolts which held the starter in place.

As the afternoon wore on, the starter removal job progressed slowly. Connell began to notice that pieces of ham were disappearing from the wing top. He decided that the other members of the crew were either getting courageous, or desperate, and tried a piece himself. He wondered how the sun had "improved the flavor so much."

By late afternoon a general feeling of pessimism and depression was setting in caused largely by hunger and thirst. The constant pitching and rolling of the plane added to the problem, and as the seas continued to build during the afternoon the situation became worse. Pope asked Connell how he had happened to pick such a deserted section of the Pacific in which to land. Connell answered in an unconcerned way, "They'll find us. If a Navy ship doesn't, then a merchant ship will. After all, we're right in the middle of the shipping lane." Connell's response was typical of both officers during the entire ordeal. No matter how bad things looked, or how they might have felt, they always were optimistic and attempted to cheer the others up.

As the sea conditions deteriorated, Rodgers reluctantly ordered the remaining fabric cut away from the lower wings. It had to be done; the port wing was starting to buckle and the already damaged starboard wing was being further weakened. Rodgers had no more thoughts about flying to Hawaii. They were going to be on the water longer than they had expected.

The fabric was cut away carefully so that the pieces were large enough to rig between the upper and lower wings as square sails. Such sails were bent on between the outer and inner wing struts and lashed with heavy waxed cord known as white line.

Next, the crew set to work strengthening the damaged rear spars. The outer ends of the lower wings were supported with manila line which ran to the tops of the outer wing struts. The damaged spars were splinted using engine brace rods and leftover antenna wire.[24]

Removing the Aeromarine starter, cutting away the wing fabric, and strengthening the weakened lower wings consumed all their energy. Hunger, thirst, and fatigue were already starting

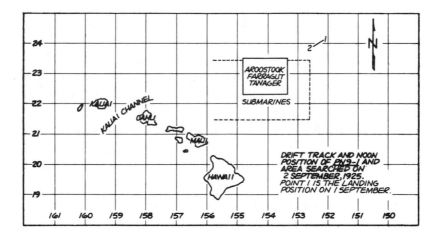

to take their toll. Still, the day's exertions had raised morale by giving the men a feeling that they could save themselves through their own efforts.

Morale received even a bigger boost that night as the exhausted crew was preparing for their third night on the water. Just after dark, Stantz copied a message from the *Aroostook*, "Cheer up John, we'll get you." In fact, the message raised a false hope. At that moment there was not the remotest possibility that they would be rescued in the next several hours—or even days.

Since 0200 that morning, the *Aroostook*, *Farragut*, and *Tanager* had shifted the search to a rectangular area west and north of the plane. The eastern limit of the new search area was along longitude 156 degrees, but the *PN9–1* had not even reached longitude 154 degrees. Overestimation of drift was the reason for the search being too far west. The day before, the *Farragut* had established the search area on the basis of an 8-knot drift and the *Aroostook* had done the same.[25]

The search west of longitude 156 degrees and north of latitude 23 degrees 43 minutes continued until 2030 hours on 3 September at which time the three ships moved south to the entrance of Kauai Channel. The *Aroostook*'s captain wanted to prevent the plane from drifting through the channel and into the open sea beyond the islands. His deployment of surface vessels and submarines on the second day, 3 September, had been done to prevent passage of the plane north or south of Kauai. He now considered that the Kauai Channel itself had not been covered. Reducing the drift estimate to 5 knots, he calculated that the plane might enter the channel sometime on 4 September.[26]

As the ships moved southward toward the channel entrance, a report was received that the USS *Whippoorwill* had sighted flares to the northward of the Kauai Channel at latitude 22 degrees 08 minutes, longitude 158 degrees 12 minutes. The *Farragut* was dispatched at high speed to investigate. One hour later the *Whippoorwill* again reported flares near the Kauai Channel entrance. The *Farragut* searched the area but found nothing. What they had thought were flares was really the planet Venus.[27]

With sundown on 3 September the general optimism about an early rescue, which had been shared by the searchers and the lost airmen, began to dwindle. It was replaced starting on the third day, 4 September, with growing pessimism. The decision to remove the lower wing fabric was the first sign of this change.

The sails, which had been made from the wing fabric, were a sign of an even deeper pessimism. By the afternoon of the second day, Rodgers, at least, recognized that rescue would be a result of their own efforts rather than simply a matter of surviving until they were found by the searching vessels. Out of this initial pessimism grew a determination and a will to survive which was shared by every member of the crew. Their problem was simple. Without food and water they could not hope to survive very long. They were 450 miles from Hawaii and drifting slowly westward towards the islands at the rate of about 1 knot. Rigged with crude sails, the seaplane would double that speed and might even make 3 knots. The difference was life or death. On the night of 3 September 1925, therefore, the crew resolved to sail the *PN9–1* to Hawaii.

V

Determination and Despair
4–7 September 1925

"HOPE IS DIMINISHING," was the gloomy headline on 4 September 1925, and in even bolder type, "PRIDE OF THE NAVY IS NOW TANGLED WRECKAGE."[1] Readers were told that the search was being carried out vigorously, but that hope for success was fading. The other side of the paper was devoted to listing the dead and injured in the *Shenandoah* crash. For the first time the two disasters became associated with one another in the public's mind. Together, they gave naval aviation a black eye.

After opening on that gloomy note, the press expanded on the earlier report that the search was continuing. The implication was that vast swarms of ships were involved in the search. "ENTIRE FLEET IN PACIFIC ORDERED TO HUNT AVIATORS."[2] The headline looked good but the reality was something else.

Out of ten guardships only three, aided by a few submarines and the USS *Whippoorwill*, were involved in the search during the first three days. The seven ships stationed east of the *Farragut* were released from their stations on 3 September, but none of them could immediately join the search. The *William Jones* was still in San Francisco. The *McCawley*, *Corry*, *Meyer*, and *Doyen*, their fuel supply nearly exhausted, had to return to San Francisco before starting to search. The next two ships down the line, the *Langley* and *Reno*, were headed toward the search area, but the *Reno*, also short of fuel, had to break off and go into Pearl Harbor. The destroyer was able to join the hunt on 5 September and the carrier finally became effective on 6 September. Coming from Australia were eighteen destroyers returning from fleet maneuvers. They could not participate in the search for several days. When they did, their efforts were concentrated on the southwest side of the islands.

During the night of 3–4 September, the *Aroostook, Tanager*, and *Farragut* had moved farther westward to cover the Kauai Channel and its entrance. They were again estimating the *PN9–1*'s drift rate at 8 knots. The *Farragut* made a second search of areas in which the *Whippoorwill* had reported seeing flares, while the *Whippoorwill*, starting at the estimated point from which the flares had come, followed the assumed plane along a 6-knot drift circle. During the day of 4 September, the *Aroostook* and *Tanager* searched down the Kauai Channel, including the areas immediately south of Kauai.[3]

The *Aroostook*'s concern that the plane might drift down the Kauai Channel and out into the open sea west of the islands was well founded and was shared by Rodgers. This problem, however, would not present itself to Rodgers and his crew for another five days.

The immediate concern of the airmen on the morning of 4 September was to get their transmitter working. The propeller had been pulled off the wind-driven generator and the heavy starter motor and flywheel were out of the engine. The next step was to couple the starter motor and flywheel to the generator shaft. Coupling the two units proved to be less a problem than securing the starter motor and flywheel in place.[4]

The wind-driven generator was mounted on a pedestal attached to the lower wing behind the port engine. The front half of the generator assembly poked between two struts which formed a "V" where they joined the lower wing. Once the propeller and its guard had been removed, there were about six inches of shaft to which they intended to attach the starter motor and flywheel.

The big problem was how to hold the heavy motor and flywheel in place. The only material available was fifty feet of wire rope which had been found in a spares locker. With this the starter motor and flywheel were lashed to one of the engine foundations, directly in front of the generator. Following this they were coupled to the generator with rubber hose and hose clamps.

The men first tried to use the starter battery to drive the starter motor. The sudden torque was too much for the hose coupling to handle, however, causing it to twist and slip. The fact that the wire rope lashings were not tight enough to hold the starter motor in place added to the problem. After several attempts, the idea of using the battery to spin the starter motor was abandoned.

Bowlin fashioned a hand crank with which to replace the starter motor on the end of the starter flywheel. The motor eliminated, the three crewmen tried to hold the flywheel in place while Connell furiously turned the crank. The high torque problem was eliminated but the system was too wobbly. The best they could turn was about 1,000 rpm, but at least 2,500 rpm were needed to generate enough power to transmit.

For most of the day, they continued to try to get the radio generator working. But by afternoon, it was apparent that the starter motor and flywheel method was not going to work. Disappointed and disgusted, they gave up. Influencing their decision to stop was another immediate problem.

The sea was now rougher than it had been the day before. The plane was yawing and coming partially broadside to the waves. The hull was standing up well but the men were concerned about the wings and wingtip pontoons. If the wingtip pontoons were carried away, the plane would lose lateral stability and capsize.

Pope and Connell decided to try using the ailerons and rudder to hold the bow into the wind. They reasoned that the wind blowing across the control surface might be enough to offer some control. After some trial and error, the technique was found to be successful. But the pilots soon learned that over control was just as bad as no control. If the controls were used to their full extent the plane tended to turn broadside to the oncoming waves. When this happened, whichever pontoon was to windward took a terrible pounding. Steering proved to be much more difficult in rough seas, which continued for the next several days.

After they had the steering technique worked out they discovered that with the sails the plane could be steered 5 degrees on either side of the wind.[5] Being able to alter their course even this small amount improved their chances for saving themselves. Rodgers could now plan in advance the strategy to avoid being blown helplessly through the slot between Oahu and Kauai.

From this time on, the pilot's seat had always to be manned, worsening the already serious problem of fatigue. There were now three watch positions to be manned; the constant radio watch being kept by Stantz and Bowlin, the night watch for ships, and now the steering watch. The job of lookout and helmsman could not be combined because of the attention required to keep the *PN9–1* on course.[6]

The food that had been intended for the in-flight meals had either been eaten, tossed into the bilge, or thrown overboard. That evening the emergency provisions were opened. Connell opened the crackers first. But instead of rationing them, he left them in the open container, available to anyone who wanted them. As the crackers were the only food the hungry men had to eat, they quickly consumed them all. Connell later remarked that he should have rationed the food. "However," he said, "we were so sure that we were going to be picked up, that although

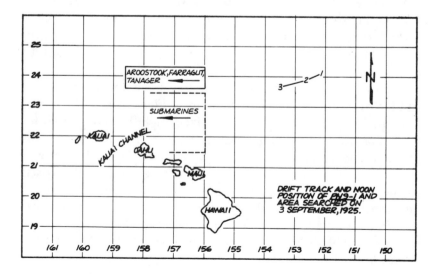

we conserved water, we didn't worry about how long the crackers would last."[7]

Later in the same evening, the canned corned beef, known as "Canned Willie," was opened. Now, however, Connell carefully rationed the amount given each man. Since this was done just after the crackers had been passed around without any thought to rationing, the change seems odd. Maybe the rough seas and general discomfort made them less optimistic. In any event, the two incidents show that while the men had not entirely given up hope of being found, they were beginning to have their doubts.

A paper drinking cup was used to measure out each man's ration, which consisted of one cupful. The corned beef tasted good but proved to be a very poor choice as an emergency ration. The heavily salted beef created tremendous thirst.

As night came on, the wind and seas increased to such an extent that Rodgers ordered the sails taken in and a sea anchor put out. The rough weather and the wild motion of the plane made the entire crew apprehensive. Pope later recalled, "Every time a sea hit the wings we all jumped out and looked at the wings, believing they had been torn off." The strain caused by uncertainty and fatigue was beginning to tell. Morale was dropping fast. During the night, the *Reno*, en route to Pearl Harbor for fuel, passed within twenty-five miles of the *PN9–1*.[8] Had Rodgers and his men known it, they would have felt even worse.

On Saturday, 5 September, the newspapers were full of new reports and suppositions. Rumors, hoaxes, and flare sightings filled the front page. With so much activity being reported, the public generally felt that the elusive *PN9–1* must be in the area of the searching ships.

The news item that offered the most hope was the reported flare sighting by the *Whippoorwill* on the night of 3 September. Captain Moses was quoted, "There is a ray of hope in the telegram which [the] *Whippoorwill* sent, that it had seen a white flare and two flares and rockets."

The report added that flight headquarters in San Francisco had calculated that if the *PN9–1* had drifted to the point from which the flares were reported, the distance covered would have indicated a drift of 5½ knots. Captain Moses was again quoted: "If the plane had drifted as far as the Kauai Channel it would be virtually intact and its wings in the air. Otherwise it would not have that drifting speed."[9]

Moses was, of course, quite right. Had the *PN9–1* actually been the source of the mysterious flares, her minimum drift rate would have been 5½ knots. Moses was also correct in assuming that had she achieved this drift rate she would have been intact. What is hard to understand is how the Navy could have used such a high drift rate as the basis for the search.

Private sailboats that sailed from San Francisco to Hawaii made the trip in about nineteen days.[10] In addition to being affected by wind conditions, their underwater profile and water-line length were major factors in determining their speed.

The sailboats, unlike the *PN9–1*, were designed to use the wind for their motive power. Even rigged with crude square sails and sailing before the wind, there was little chance that the *PN9–1* could have achieved the sailing efficiency of a well-designed sailboat. Her natural tendency was to lay bow to the wind so that her hull, wings, and tail presented their minimum surface area to the wind.

In 1925, private sailboats traveling to Hawaii from San Francisco were not the common occurrence they are today. On the

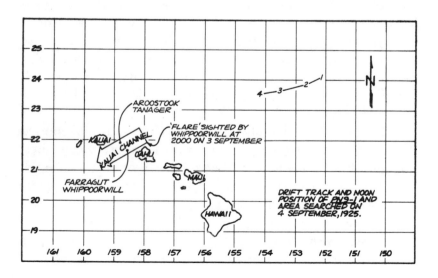

other hand, this trip made by commercial ships under sail was a well-recorded fact and was still occuring in 1925. Therefore, the Navy had numerous examples of the speed at which wind-driven vessels might be expected to travel. They could have used any ship of the Spreckles sugar packet fleet, for example.

Even at best, the fast sugar packets that regularly made the run between San Francisco and the islands averaged 8 to 10 knots. Typical of this class was the three-masted schooner *Emma Claudia*. She made the San Francisco-to-Hilo run in a blistering eight days and eight hours. Her average speed on this record-making run was just over 10 knots.[11] It is hard to understand how anyone could have thought that the *PN9–1* could have maintained an average speed of even half that figure once she was on the water and without engines.

In 1925, the Navy must certainly have been aware of the three factors that comprised open-sea drift. They are sea current, wind-driven current, and leeway. The sea current in the area where the *PN9–1* went down is generally 270 degrees, true, at .2 to .3 knots. The wind-driven current is difficult to estimate because the prevailing winds vary in that area during that time of year. Leeway, the last factor, is usually the hardest to compute accurately.

In 1978 the problem of estimating the *PN9–1*'s drift was presented to the United States Coast Guard in San Francisco. In dealing with the problem Lieutenant J. J. Hathaway wrote:

> The Coast Guard has had little experience with drifting sea-planes and consequently we have not compiled drift data on them. Having no wind data or leeway characteristics for the seaplane, I would still hazard a guess that the total drift of a seaplane even with makeshift sails, would not exceed 2 or 3½ knots.[12]

In 1925 the Navy also had little experience with drifting seaplanes and certainly no compiled drift data and leeway characterics. Still, their experience with vessels adrift at sea could reasonably be assumed to be as great as that of the Coast Guard. Yet they overestimated the *PN9–1*'s drift to be 5 to 8 knots.

Credit must be given to the *Aroostook*'s captain for his appraisal of the danger that the *PN9–1* might slip past the searchers and down the Kauai Channel. Probably for this reason alone he based his search on an estimated drift rate of 8 knots. More than anything else, he wanted to guard against the chance that Rodgers and his men would perish in the open sea beyond the islands. It could also be argued that with the limited resources at his disposal he had no other choice.[13]

While the *Aroostook* and *Farragut* plowed the seas west of Kauai, AP was dispelling rumors at home and reporting a hoax. The search for the *PN9–1*, so close to the islands, had made coast watching there a popular pastime and hardly a day passed when some "sighting" was not reported.

Late in the afternoon on 4 September, Navy headquarters at Pearl Harbor was swamped with reports that a sampan had the *PN9–1* in tow off Waiana. The Navy soon learned that the plane was a similar appearing F–5L which, after being under tow for a short while, took off again. The affair seemed unimportant and the Navy did not report it to the press. AP, however, needed news and when the incident came to light they made the most of it. Their lead read, "Hopes that the *PN9–1*, missing naval seaplane, had been discovered and was being towed to Honolulu, were dissipated tonight when it was discovered that the plane in question was a patrol craft from Pearl Harbor."

Readers on the mainland, who had not previously read a report that the *PN9–1* might be under tow, did not have any hopes to be dissipated. They were more interested in the next story which described a clumsy hoax first reported by a Florida resident.

Arthur Alman, an amateur radio operator in St. Augustine, Florida, told the local newspapers that he had been in contact with the USS *Lynchburg*, which was then with the Battle Fleet destroyers in the Pacific. The operator aboard the *Lynchburg* supposedly told Alman that they were 400 miles south of Samoa and that the *PN9–1* had been found. The crew was described as being in good health. The report was unclear as to whether the crew was supposed to be aboard the *Lynchburg* or whether their having been found was simply being reported.

Alman gave this story to the *Augustine Record*, which passed it on to AP. The story seemed believable at the time, but AP had the good sense to check with the Navy before releasing it. The news agency quickly learned that there was no USS *Lynchburg*. The Navy also pointed out that "if the ship with which Alman talked was with the Pacific Fleet, the position given should have been several miles north of Samoa."[14] Whether Alman made the whole thing up or was himself the victim of a hoax is not known. One fact, however, was certain—nobody knew where the *PN9–1* was.

On 5 September, while west coast Americans read the morning paper and followed with intense interest the search for the *PN9–1*, Rodgers and his crew were starting another uncomfortable day. False sightings and hoaxes may, or may not, have interested them. Certainly, the presence of two fifteen-foot tiger sharks following their wake caught their attention.

Pope was sitting in the pilot's seat "flying the plane," when he saw Rodgers stick his head out of the forward cockpit. The rumpled captain searched the horizon forward and then looked aft. He spotted the sharks. "Good morning strangers."

Pope wondered to whom Rodgers was talking and asked, "who's that?"

"Here's a couple of playmates for you, Pope—some tiger sharks," answered Rodgers.

Connell, hearing the exchange, climbed onto the hull through the engineer's cockpit and looked around trying to discover what Rodgers and Pope were talking about. He saw the sharks which were now swimming lazily near the bow and thought to himself. "You'll wait a long time before you gain anything from following this craft." Whether Connell was referring to their shortage of food or the strength of the duralumin hull is not recorded.

This was not the first time that they had seen sharks in their wake. Since the first day Rodgers had noted dozens of smaller sharks round the plane. These two, however, were the largest by far. They were a grim reminder of what could happen to men who were lost at sea.

After the sharks had been sighted, Rodgers disappeared back into the hull. Connell also pulled his head back in and was surprised to see his captain crawling around on his hands and knees. Connell wondered what he was doing. Rodgers seemed to be working on something on the deck, first with his right hand and then with his left. Connell shifted his body forward to where Rodgers was working. He saw that Rodgers was trying to dig out a piece of crust from one of the sandwiches which someone had thrown into the bilge. Shortly, the commander's efforts were rewarded. The piece he got was about thumb nail size. As Rodgers popped the crumb in his mouth he saw Connell watching him. Neither man said anything. Rodgers grinned and went out through the navigator's cockpit.

Every man aboard the *PN9–1* knew that if they were to be found they would have to tell the searchers where they were. To do that they needed a transmitter. The issue was discussed and all agreed there was no hope of using the radio generator. How, then, could they transmit if they had no way to power the radio? The storage batteries were sufficient to operate the receiver but not adequate for the transmitter. The wind-driven generator had defied their best efforts. The best qualified man aboard to answer the question was the radioman, Stantz. He did not let them down. Stantz suggested that a spark set could be rigged from the transmitter and ignition parts. Primitive though the solution was, there seemed to be a better chance of getting a message out that way than through continuing to try to get the regular transmitter working.

The SE1085 transmitter was disassembled to obtain the loading coils, condensers, and other parts necessary to build the spark set. Bowlin removed the ignition coil and distributor from the already partially cannibalized starboard engine, and a twelve-volt ignition battery was used for the source of power. The "Rube Goldberg" set was hooked up so that the make and break in the primary circuit of the ignition coil was accomplished by rotating the distributor head. Again, the starter flywheel was used, this time to turn the distributor shaft.[15]

When Stantz and Bowlin had completed building the set, the antenna was strung from the radio cockpit, over the upper wing and down to the bow. While Pope, Bowlin, and Connell watched, Stantz sent out his first SOS and position report. Con-

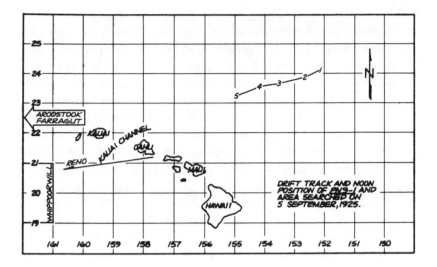

nell later said the thing they had built looked more "like a static machine than a spark set. It threw a spark which looked as though it would transmit a message around the world."

While Stantz was pounding out his message, Bowlin climbed up on the hull and touched the antenna to satisfy himself that the contraption was "putting out." Everyone was startled when a large blue spark arced from the wire to Bowlin's finger. Bowlin, who was nearly knocked off the plane, concluded that the set was indeed "putting out."

Further proof came just a few minutes later. Stantz was steadily sending out an SOS followed by their position report and drift rate. Rodgers was forward in the navigator's cockpit going over his charts. He stopped what he was doing and started to climb up on the bow. As he did the back of his neck touched the antenna. The jolt he received knocked him back into the hull. When he recovered he shouted down the hull to the surprised crew, "I don't think there's much doubt about that thing putting out." Despite the spectacular demonstrations of its voltage, the set only reached out about ten miles.[16] There was no one close enough to hear them.

Their situation was growing desperate. The first two or three days had not been too hard on them physically. During that time there had been enough food and water to at least keep them going. Their natural energy reserves had also helped. Up to this point only Stantz had suffered serious physical sickness. Their belief that rescue was just a short time away also helped. By sundown on 5 September, their fourth day adrift, these resources had pretty well been used up.

Pope understated the situation when he said, "We were beginning to get tired of being rocked in the plane so long in such cramped quarters and with so little food." Morale was dropping rapidly as the airmen heard that the search was working farther west. Their only hope, other than a chance rescue by a passing steamer, seemed to be the *Langley* and her planes. By the evening of 5 September the carrier was on station "V" and was preparing to assume operational control of the search at 0800 the following morning.[17] They had some comfort in knowing that the *Langley* was behind them and would be searching westward.

By now almost all the food aboard was gone. Some of it, in the form of orange peels and cast-off, partially eaten sandwiches, lay rotting in the bilges. The hardtack, which next to the oranges had been the most edible, was also gone. The only food remaining was the "Canned Willie" which was too strong to eat. Even when the ration was reduced to a half cup the salty meat caused nausea and unquenchable thirst. The commander explained their situation. "It was found impossible to eat the corned beef, which created desire for water. All endeavors to digest the corned beef caused violent nausea."

Food, however, was really a secondary problem. More serious was the shortage of water. On the fourth day they still had a small amount left which was being rationed very carefully. The amount allowed to them each day, however, was far below the minimum needed to maintain strength and health. Compounding these problems was the extreme fatigue they all suffered. The uneasy motion of the plane, the poor accommodations, and the need to divide several watch assignments among five men all prevented them from sleeping.

Stantz and Bowlin stood the radio watches. Because of his growing weakness and his proficiency with the radio, Stantz was spared the other assignments. This offered him no respite, however, because he was almost continuously at the radio. Bowlin shared with the others the lookout and steering watches, and relieved Stantz on the radio watch. The steering watch, manned twenty-four hours a day and often requiring intense concentration by the man at the wheel, was the worst. The situation was not so bad when the weather was moderate. But when the seas were heavy or the wind strong, all the helmsman's efforts were required to keep the plane on course, and, more importantly, to keep the strain on the wing pontoons to a minimum.

That night, while Rodgers worked on his charts plotting the position of the searching ships, a flying fish came aboard. The fish came through the navigator's hatch and landed flopping on the deck at Rodger's feet. The sudden activity in the navigator's cockpit alerted the rest of the crew. Stantz was monitoring the radio and sending out their position reports when the fish came aboard. Pope was in the pilot's seat where he spent most of his time. He had become the most proficient at steering the plane on the water and stood that watch more than anybody else. Connell and Bowlin were sitting between the engines watching for lights or some other sign of rescue.

After he caught the flopping, slippery fish Rodgers stood up in the navigator's cockpit. "Look what I got," he called to the others. At first the others failed to grasp that Rodgers intended to eat the fish. Only after he had cut up and eaten part of the fish, did the others consent to sample a piece. They decided that raw fish was not too bad.

The fish had apparently been attracted by the light over the chart table. Hoping to lure more flying fish aboard, the four-volt instrument light from a steering compass was rigged near the waterline at the radio door. Several hours passed but no fish came aboard. Late that night they gave up and disconnected the light. There was still nothing to eat.

"MITCHELL THROWS BOMB INTO RANKS OF WAR BUREAUS" was the top news story on 6 September 1925.[18] The nation's leading advocate for an independent air force had publicly attacked both the War and Navy Departments in a scathing statement made to the press. He described the apparent loss of the *PN9–1* and the recent crash of the USS *Shenandoah* as a "frightful aeronautical accident and loss of life, equipment and treasure. . . ." Then he dropped his bombshell. "These accidents are the direct result of the incompetence, criminal negligence, and almost treasonable administration of the national defense by the Navy and War Departments."

Following this shocking opener was his usual argument in support of an independent air force, as well as his usual attack on the Navy. Mitchell assailed the West Coast-Hawaii Seaplane Flight directly:

> Next, to get publicity and make a noise about what it was doing with aircraft, this so-called Hawaiian Flight was arranged for. Even if it had been successful to Honolulu it would have meant little, either commercially or strategically, compared to what a flight to Europe or Asia would. Three airplanes were built to participate in it. These showed nothing novel in design and were untried for this kind of work. One never got away from the Pacific Coast, another flew a few miles out and was forced to land in the water, and one was lost on the high seas.
>
> Patrol vessels were stationed every two hundred miles, a distance entirely too far apart for an experimental flight of this kind. With such primitive flying machines as the PN9's are, double or triple this number of vessels should have been there. In fact the whole Pacific Fleet should have been employed there. Instead of joyriding around the Antipodes. As it was, when these slow moving airplanes, going about seventy-five miles per hour, were first sighted from the destroyers they should have steamed in the direction the airplane was going. This would not only indicate the proper course to the plane but would place the destroyer closer in the case of accident. As the airplanes were only moving at about seventy-five miles per hour, a destroyer could have been speeded up to within thirty miles of that speed.
>
> Why, if they expected to run short of fuel, as indeed they might, did they not make arrangements for refueling the airplane while it was in the air by another airplane as we have repeatedly done? Why did they carry a crew of five when the weight of two men in fuel might have carried the ship through.

What happened to this really good-for-nothing big, lumbering flying boat when its brave navigator began to run short of gas over a heavy sea? The probability is that they held her up as long as they could. As they neared the water, caught by a sudden gust, she might have been thrown into a stall and gone down straight under the waves. Hope that some passing fisherman may have picked them up as Lieutenant Wade was picked up in the North Sea. Our Navy did not find him either, all they did was to smash his plane when it was turned over to them by the fisherman. After all, the Hawaiian Islands are not a vital area with our present methods of national defense.

Next in line for criticism was the *Shenandoah*'s flight. "The *Shenandoah* was going west on a propaganda mission for the Navy to offset the adverse publicity caused by failures in the Pacific." If there were people who had yet failed to associate the Pacific flight failure with the *Shenandoah* crash, Mitchell did that for them. But the *Shenandoah* crash was a closed affair—the search for the *PN9–1* was a continuing drama.

"HONOLULU OFFICIALS CLING TO HOPE THAT FIVE AVIATORS WILL BE SAVED." News about Rodgers and his crew was limited to a half column below Colonel Mitchell's picture. The headline and the lack of news reflected the growing fear that the men would not be found alive.[19]

The same newspaper reported that the Japanese Fisherman's Association had offered to send "several fast fishing sampans" to assist in the search. The offer was declined by the Navy official in Hawaii who said that there were already so many fast ships and airplanes engaged in the search that use of the fishing boats would "only be an unnecessary expense to the Japanese." Nevertheless, the fishermen promised to report any unusual lights or wreckage. The Navy's rejection of the fishermen's offer was not based on the fact that there were already too many ships or that the Japanese would incur unnecessary expense. The Navy was simply being diplomatic in saying no. It may have had several reasons for turning down the offer of assistance, some of them legitimate and others less so.

There is no doubt that the Navy was shorthanded during the search, but integrating the Japanese fishing boats into the operation would have been difficult, if not impossible. The major roadblock was communications. Most of the Japanese fishing boats were without radios and there was a language problem, since most of the fishermen spoke only Japanese. Unless the Japanese fishing boats could have been brought into the Navy radio net, there would have been no practical way to direct their search efforts.

Another factor may have been the growing anti-Japanese feeling. Japan was fast becoming a major naval rival in the Pacific. The Navy's pride may have been pricked to think that a Japanese fisherman might succeed where the American Navy might fail. On the other hand, if the fishermen happened upon the plane during the normal exercise of their profession, the Navy's loss of face would be considerably less. It was therefore more attractive to accept their cooperation in reporting unusual lights and wreckage than to assign them actively to the search.

The only other AP article about the plane on that day was a brief rehash of the 5 September search operations. Included was a report that officers in Honolulu were still hopeful that the men would be found alive. Reference was made to a Lieutenant Locatelli who in 1924 drifted for several days in the North Sea until he was rescued by an American Navy vessel. To further hearten the readers, AP quoted officers in Honolulu as having "pointed out that the seaplane was stocked with sufficient water

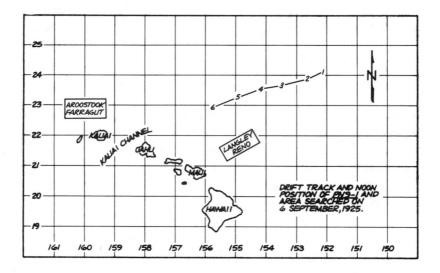

to keep five men alive indefinitely and that they could, if necessary, survive without food for several days."[20]

Rodgers and his men might have wondered where that infinite supply of water was hidden aboard their plane. Not only were they down to the two reserve canteens that Rodgers had been keeping, but it was also evident they would have to survive without food for several days. They had tried to catch fish with a bent wire hook, but their makeshift, baitless hook proved unattractive to the fish, and after several fruitless hours the airmen gave up.

Stantz had temporarily recovered from his seasickness, and motivated by real hunger he tried again to eat the "Canned Willie." The attempt was an awful mistake. The nausea he suffered was the worst yet, convincing the others that the corned beef was not a solution to their hunger problem. After that, no attempt was made to eat the "Canned Willie."[21]

Weakness caused by dehydration, hunger, and lack of sleep was now a serious problem. Keeping awake while standing watch on deck or in the pilot's seat was a major effort. Moving around for even a short time necessitated a rest, and the men were reduced to crawling from place to place. In such a weakened state, the pitching of the plane increased the danger that one of them would go overboard. To guard against this a lifeline was run from the bow to the tail. Movement along the top of the hull was done hanging onto the line. At night the man on watch was made fast with a line to one of the frames inside the hull.[22]

The sea was so rough on the night of 6–7 September that they had to take in the sails and put out a bucket as a makeshift sea anchor. The job was extremely hazardous and difficult. The waves, breaking over the skeleton of the lower wings, made footing hard to find. Fatigue and the wild motion of the plane added to the danger as they worked.

While the sails were being taken in, Stantz, who was monitoring the radio, copied a message from the *Aroostook*. "We'll get you yet. Use very stars. Hammer hull so submarines will hear on oscillators." When the others tumbled below after wrestling with the sails, Stantz showed Rodgers the message, who read it out loud. Pope and Bowlin immediately scrambled into the engineer's compartment where there was a hammer in the tool box. Bowlin was digging in the tool box when Pope remembered that there was another hammer in the engine tool kit. They both returned to the radio room and started pounding on the hull with a vengeance. Their enthusiasm was so great that Stantz was afraid they might knock a hole in the hull.

The effort, of course, was wasted. There was no submarine close enough to hear them just as there was no ship near enough to pick up Stantz's SOS and position reports. Rodgers made no attempt to stop them. It was better that they have hope and something to do.

The violent motion of the plane and the noise of the waves hitting the hull made them all miserable. Connell remarked later, "it was a great wonder that we all were not seasick." Connell was able to sleep, however, and said he was doing so soundly when he was awakened by Rodgers yelling "rain, rain." The shout brought everyone out. But the men were frustrated in trying to take advantage of the shower by the fact that they had laid out the sails with the fabric's unpainted side up. The light shower was completely absorbed by the fabric and no water was saved. The desperate and disappointed men resorted to licking the fabric and hull for what little moisture they could get.

Occasionally, throughout the night, Pope and Bowlin pounded on the hull. The disappointment seems to have been felt most keenly by Stantz, who by this time was very weak. He described the following days as being "just one long day."

At 0800 on 6 September, the *Langley* assumed command of the search. The *Aroostook* was directed to continue searching in the vicinity and to the northward of Kauai.[23] After searching along the windward shore of Molakai and Maui, the *Farragut* moved into the Alenuihaha Channel between Maui and Hawaii.[24] The *Reno*, having refueled, was ordered to join the *Langley* east of Maui for plane guard duty.[25] All the original search ships were now short of fuel and plans had already been made to send them into Pearl Harbor. Those ships that were lowest on fuel were sent in first. The *Whippoorwill* entered Pearl Harbor at 0700.

At 1545 both the *Farragut* and *Aroostook* received the electrifying report that an inter-island steamer had spotted a seaplane drifting in the Kauai Channel, about five miles offshore. Both ships were sent to the scene as fast as they could go. They needed no urging. The *Aroostook*, whose bottom was very foul, wheezed along at her maximum 14 knots.[26] The leaner, healthier *Farragut* charged toward the scene at 24 knots.[27] In the meantime two F–5L seaplanes from Pearl Harbor were also sent to investigate. They arrived in the area well ahead of the two ships and after a short search found the "plane" that the steamer had sighted—an abandoned sampan.[28]

Despite the report sent back by the planes, the *Farragut* and *Aroostook* continued their high speed runs into the area. The destroyer arrived at 1844 and the *Aroostook*, which had been closer, was only fifteen minutes behind her. The two ships searched the area for an hour and a half before heading toward Pearl Harbor to refuel.[29]

While other ships searched the area north and west of the island, the *Langley* and her planes covered an area to the east. The carrier was acting on information supplied by the *Aroostook* which indicated that the area east of Maui between longitudes 152 degrees and 156 degrees had received scant attention. The planes carried by the *Langley* were not equipped with floats and there was concern about the possibility of losing both plane and pilot if one went down. Therefore, in consideration of safety, the sound decision was made to use only two planes at a time, searching within sight of each other.[30]

The air search lasted until sunset. After the last pair of search planes had been recovered, the carrier and her guardship retired southward. Tomorrow's search, the sixth day, was to start from a point twenty-three miles south.

On Monday, 7 September, the *PN9–1* received only a half column on the front page. The reason was obvious—there was nothing to report. The entire article was devoted to the misidentification of the derelict sampan on the previous day. There was no speculation about the fate of Rodgers and his crew and no optimistic statement from Navy officials. The opinion that the five men were probably dead had not yet been expressed openly. That such an opinion was growing, however, was evident from the sparse coverage.

The growing pessimism of the press was understandable. Their sources of information were the operations centers in San Francisco and Pearl Harbor. The search was now nearly a week old with no clue to the *PN9–1*'s fate. Navy officers, fully aware of the multitude of problems associated with a forced landing at sea, were beginning to have doubts. Those doubts, though not explicitly stated, were conveyed to the newsmen.

Captain W. Van Auken, commanding the *Aroostook*, prepared a lengthy report on 7 September. In his report he gave his views on the operation to date and concluded with a grim speculation:

> Considering all attendant circumstances and radio messages, it is not understood why radio communication ceased without warning at 1607 between the plane and [the] *Aroostook* without even a sign of SOS, and where the plane was about to land. Also, considering that the plane could not make out the dense smoke of [the] *Aroostook* with exceptional visibility all around the horizon, it is believed that the plane must have been over twenty miles, at least, from [the] *Aroostook*, when the radio communications ceased. As the plane was in a rain squall during the last minute of communication with [the] *Aroostook*, and as gasoline was about gone, it is possible that the plane in landing without motors was damaged. It is the Commanding Officer's opinion that if the plane or personnel were not damaged or injured that some message of a forced landing could, and would have been, transmitted before, or after, the plane was on the water. Also, that if the plane were not damaged, with the sea experience of Commander Rodgers, the plane would have been kept afloat, and its course and drift so regulated that it could not pass unseen through any of the channels of the Hawaiian Islands, with which Commander Rodgers was so well acquainted. It is further believed that if the plane remained afloat, equipped as it was for an extended expedition, the personnel could remain fairly comfortable and exist for over a week. But if visibility in the rain squall were bad, combined with the nervous tension of the pilots at that time, after twenty-four hours in the air, worry over gasoline shortage, it is possible that a sudden loss of motors with a tail wind in a moderate, choppy sea might have caused a nose dive upon landing. In this unfortunate event, it is probable that with a damaged

pontoon and injured personnel the plane went down or remained partially submerged.[31]

Clearly, the captain believed the five men were dead. He
based his opinion on two points: the *Aroostook* had received no
radio message after 1607 on 1 September and the plane had not
been seen since 1 September.

With the advantage of hindsight, we now know that the
PN9–1 could not transmit and the search was being conducted
too far south and west of the plane's position. Faulty radio bearings and overestimated drift were the reasons for the latter situation. The *Aroostook*'s captain did not know about the radio
problems aboard the *PN9–1* and was unaware that the 8-knot
drift estimate was about four times the actual rate. Under the
circumstances, Captain Van Auken's opinion was justified.

Time alone was sufficient to raise doubts about their chance
for survival, but the men aboard the *PN9–1* would have taken
exception with this statement, ". . . equipped as it was for an
extended expedition, the personnel could remain fairly comfortable and exist for over a week." The extent of their expedition
was to have been twenty-six hours and nine minutes, for which
they were adequately provisioned. They had now been at sea
for six days, for which they were not adequately provisioned.

Their weakened condition was growing worse. Stantz had
lost all track of time and the others were just barely hanging on.
The little water remaining did not last through the day, and
without water they could not survive much longer.

Rodgers recalled the still his mother had given him. The
problem was that the still needed gasoline for fuel and gasoline
was something they did not have. Rodgers understated the problem when he said, "without gasoline, the operation of the still
was very difficult."[32] The fuel problem was resolved with a
decision to burn wood. But first, wood had to be obtained and
the still had to be modified to burn it.

Because the hull was built entirely of aluminum, the only
wood available was in the wings and tail. Removing wood from
the tail was out of the question. Even had they been in good
physical condition working back there would have been too dangerous. The logical choice was to take wood from the lower

wings. They were already stripped and wood could be obtained with the least effort. The lower wings, with their multitude of exposed spars and ribs, also had plenty of places to hang on to.

How much of the lower wings could be cannibalized for wood was limited by the need to keep the lower wing and wingtip floats intact. Loss of these vital components would be their undoing. Therefore, in order to maintain the structural integrity of the wing and still get enough wood to fire the still, they only took wood from the trailing edges, which on the *PN9–1* were formed by the rib ends extending beyond the after spar. With considerable effort and risk, the men crawled out onto the lower wings, broke off all the rib ends and brought them inboard.

The work was exhausting for the weakened men and frequent rests were necessary. Since there was no place to collect the wood on the wings, each piece had to be brought in as it was broken off. Crawling across the open, wave-washed wing was itself a major effort. Four men working in shifts took over three hours to break off fifty ribs.[33]

The still's gas tank and burner assembly were replaced with a metal bucket. Broken rib tips and pieces of wing fabric were put in the bucket and set afire and the still was then placed over the bucket. According to Rodgers, after five hours of "careful manipulations" one quart of fresh water was distilled. The effort used up their entire supply of fuel, and all their energy. The much needed water helped, but because of lack of strength and the need to keep the plane in one piece no second attempt was made.

Throughout the day, the *Langley* and *Reno* continued searching south of the flight path. Two of the *Langley*'s planes flew a gridiron pattern ahead of the two ships. The pattern, twelve nautical miles wide and about thirty nautical miles long, was flown for three hours. At the end of each three-hour period the two search planes were recovered and a fresh pair was launched. The operations, identical to those of the previous day, were carried out with remarkable precision and without interruptions. Notably, there were no equipment failures and fortunately no casualties. At the end of the second day the *Langley* reported that an area of 4,000 square miles had been thoroughly swept during the two-day period.[34]

On 6 September the *Aroostook* had suggested that the *Langley* search west of longitude 152 degrees "in the hope that the plane may be drifting at a speed of less than 3 knots. . . ."[35] Based on this suggestion the estimate of the *PN9*'s drift rate was reduced to 1.25 to 1.75 knots.

The *Langley* spent 6 and 7 September covering an area between longitude 154 and 156, and just above latitude 21—well south of the *PN9–1*'s actual drift track. Had she worked between the same longitudes, but farther north, along latitude 23, she would have almost certainly found the seaplane.

The *Aroostook* spent the day combing the sea north of Kauai. By this time she and her helpers had steamed over 1,367 nautical miles searching for the *PN9–1*. There had been numerous false sightings but no tangible evidence that the seaplane was still afloat. Night and day, the *Aroostook* maintained a special watch of two officers and twelve men. Even the chaplain stood watch.[36]

By the evening of 7 September the situation aboard the *PN9–1* was serious and becoming worse. Stantz was dying and his deterioration was a grim reminder to the others that unless help came soon they would all die. During the days to follow, the sufferings of their friend and fellow crewman weighed heavily on the four healthier men who increasingly suffered periods of extreme despondency.

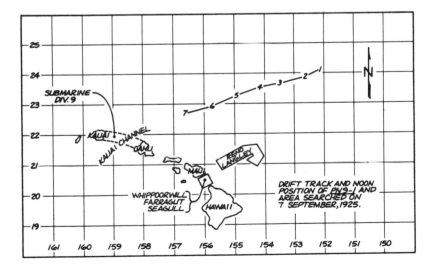

They were experiencing the first stages of starvation, but dehydration was what was killing them. Lack of water had by now become their most serious problem. The weakness resulting from the combination of thirst, hunger, and fatigue made movement about the plane increasingly slow and painful. Their hope faded and their determination showed signs of waning, but still they hung on. The men were entering the third period of their ordeal characterized by drastic fluctuations between wild hope and deep despondency. The crew of the *PN9–1* was very near the end of its rope.

VI

Rescue
8–10 September 1925

"HOPE IS GIVEN UP FOR RESCUE ALIVE OF FIVE AVIATORS." The banner headline on 8 September blurted out what most people already believed but had been reluctant to admit. The brief news article recounted the *PN9–1*'s last efforts to locate the *Aroostook* and the fruitless seven-day search for the plane that followed. Captain Moses was asked to offer some explanation about what had gone wrong. Moses said that he believed that "Rodgers traveled too fast and consumed his gasoline supplies."[1]

The original explanation, which had appeared on 2 September, attributed the excess gas consumption to heavy headwinds which had slowed the plane down. Readers, who probably had forgotten what they had read several days earlier anyway, were now told that the plane had been going too fast.

Why not admit that the trade winds had failed to develop as expected and the plane ran out of gas? Any officer connected with the flight, especially Moses, knew that was the case. To tell the truth at this time, however, was politically the wrong thing to do.

The *Shenandoah*'s loss and the *PN9–1*'s disappearance had been daily companion stories in the nation's newspapers since 4 September. The twin disasters had embarrassed the Navy at a time when it could ill afford to be embarrassed. The *PN9–1* and her crew were probably gone, but the Navy was still alive and embroiled with the Army in the battle for appropriations.

Captain Moses was no fool. In view of the uproar that had

followed Mitchell's charges, it would not have been wise to admit that the success of the flight had largely hinged on something so uncertain as the wind. A good captain looks after his ship and Moses looked after his. He attributed the failure to a combination of advanced technology and human error because this explanation would be more acceptable to the public than the truth.

The situation aboard the plane was bad and getting worse. But despite the headlines, the men were not yet finished. The one canteen of water which had been squeezed out of Rodgers's small still had already been used up. Later that day, the men tried to drink the water in the radiators. They had not done so until now because the water was known to be contaminated with "Liquid X," added to the water as a precaution against leaks. The situation was now desperate. With no water to drink and not so much as a hint of rain, the men were slowly dying of thirst. In a later comment about their situation on the seventh day, Rodgers said:

> It was apparent that there was some doubt whether we would be able to last until we reached Kauai, although we were nearing our destination. At this time it was almost impossible to move about except by crawling on our hands and knees. Stantz and Bowlin had become so weak that they could no longer man a full radio watch.[2]

At this point anything was worth a try. They drained the water from a radiator and made several attempts to strain the "Liquid X" out of the water using a 100-mesh screen, a chamois, and a piece of wing fabric. All the attempts were unsuccessful. Anyone who drank the water became ill. Rodgers later said that had the radiator compound not been added, the water supply would have been ample. What he forgot to add was that had the trade winds blown as expected, the problem would not have existed.

Morale was at its lowest point. Stantz came across a photograph of his children while rummaging through his spare parts box. His find brought on a state of deep depression and he became convinced they were not going to be found. Bowlin was also depressed thinking about his family. Orphaned as a child, he had been raised by his grandparents and an aunt. He was very close to his grandmother, and was worried that she might die from shock and grief upon hearing that he was lost at sea.[3]

Rodgers, who had a story to cover any situation, tried to keep their spirits up by telling about people who had been in similar circumstances and survived. He also stood extra watches and often gave away his food and water ration. If he felt despair, and he probably did, he kept it to himself. Rodgers was assisted by an exceptional officer. Connell was enormously well liked by the crew and, like Rodgers, always presented an optimistic face to the world. He was not a story teller, but his offhand acceptance that rescue was simply a matter of time had the same effect.

Unfortunately, the best efforts of two fine officers could not overcome the effects of thirst and starvation. Adding to their problems were the depressing radio reports that the search was being conducted in the wrong place. Rodgers in a radio speech later said:

> It took us nine days to reach our objective, and during that
> time we went through some of the experiences which are to be
> found in books describing a mariner cast away at sea. . . .
> Then we had an entirely new experience. We were as if in pur-
> gatory listening over our radio to what was going on in the
> world. We heard reports of the searching vessels, the news of
> [the] *Shenandoah*'s disaster . . . we heard ourselves consigned to
> a watery grave by our fellow aviators.[4]

Two of the messages received on 8 September had been particularly hard on morale; the order to conduct one final search and the message suggesting that the *PN9–1*'s crew were dead. Actually, Stantz had either copied only a part of the first message or had misunderstood the order to the searching vessels. In any event, the *PN9–1*'s crew believed that the search was being called off. Their gloom was partially dispelled later in the day by a message directing the searching ships to maintain station.

Until now the plane had simply been driven downwind. The jury-rigged sails helped and some directional control was achieved by use of the rudder and ailerons. But the *PN9–1* essentially followed the whim of the wind and the ocean current. On more than one occasion Rodgers had expressed to Connell

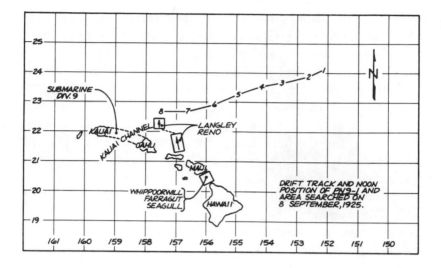

DRIFT TRACK AND NOON POSITION OF PN9-1 AND AREA SEARCHED ON 8 SEPTEMBER, 1925.

a desire to have more control over where they went, and hence, their fate.

For some time Connell had been trying to figure out a way to improve their control over the *PN9-1*'s direction. Typically, the obvious answer did not register until the problem had been around a while. When he finally hit upon the solution, Connell asked himself, "why didn't I see that before?" The solution demonstrated how useful a knowledge of seamanship could be to an aviator down at sea.

In order for a sailcraft to make way on any point of sailing, other than dead before the wind, it must have some way of offering lateral resistance to the wind's force. A keel which "hangs" down below the boat can provide such resistance. In effect, a keel is a flat wall that keeps the boat from being pushed sideways when sailing across the wind. A keel is never 100 percent effective, and every boat suffers leeway when working across or onto the wind.

Although the *PN9-1* had a keel, it was not one designed to offer lateral resistance. Any child knows that a properly designed block of wood with a nail for a mast and a square paper sail will make respectable way dead downwind. The *PN9-1* was not wholly unlike a block of wood. True, the plane could crab five degrees or so on each side of the windstream, but that was not enough. If Rodgers were to have more control over where the *PN9–1* sailed, he needed some sort of keel that offered lateral resistance.

Obviously, adding a deep keel to the centerline of the hull was an impossible task. Connell's brainstorm—the obvious answer—was to add lee boards. Lee boards are large, essentially flat plates which are attached to the sides of some sailboats. As the boat sails on or across the wind, the lee board is dropped down below the waterline and affords lateral resistance in the same way a centerline keel does.

On 8 September, Connell made lee boards from three of the flat metal floorboards in the hull. He had one lashed to the hull just aft of the radio door on the starboard side, and the other two lashed on either side of the hull under the wings. They were tied to the struts that ran from the wings to the hull. The result was about twenty square feet of keel, which showed an immediate effect. This small amount, even though relatively inefficient, allowed the plane to make 15 degrees on either side of their downwind course.

About 2200 morale was given a real boost. Pope was in the pilot's seat steering. Rodgers was on watch propped against an engine mount. The others were asleep. Suddenly Pope saw a light on the clouds low on the horizon. There was only a speck of light. He watched it for one or two minutes and when the light did not go away he called the captain. Rodgers looked and agreed that Pope did indeed see lights. Greatly heartened, Rodgers hurried below to his charts while Pope shouted for the others to wake up.

When Rodgers returned on deck he found a very excited crew. The general opinion was that the lights were the *Langley* and her escort which were known to have moved north at sunset on 7 September. Rodgers knew better. "Those are Army searchlights on Oahu," he told them.

Rodgers's revelation hardly daunted them at the time, since they had no idea how far away Oahu was. So far as they were concerned, any light that could be seen was close, and Pope excitedly predicted an early morning landing. The lights were the first sign of life they had seen since sighting the freighter on the third day, and everyone talked at once.

Rodgers knew that the lights were much farther away than they believed. He was finally able to get their attention and told them the truth. The report did not make any difference to Pope, who later said, "I felt good that night thinking we would hit Pearl Harbor." Rodgers felt good too. In his official report he wrote, "their position checked with my navigation, which was very encouraging." In a later speech to the National Aeronautics Association he said, "It checked with my navigation all right, which was more relief to me than it was to anybody else I think."[5] The airmen literally saw a light at the end of the tunnel.

While the men were still discussing the lights, Rodgers asked Connell to come with him to the navigator's cockpit. When the two officers were alone Rodgers pointed out that their present position indicated that they would probably pass through the Kauai Channel between Oahu and Kauai. Even with Connell's lee boards, there was virtually no hope of making Oahu. The goal would probably have to be the more distant Kauai.

Thursday, without water and having received two depressing messages, had been a bad day for all of them. Sighting the lights on Oahu had made a big difference, and neither Rodgers nor Connell wanted to take that away. Stantz, Bowlin, and Pope fully expected to be in Oahu in a fairly short time. The two officers agreed to say nothing about the situation that night.

Throughout the trip, Rodgers was concerned with three problems. The first was to insure that the wing pontoons held together. This had been accomplished by stripping away the wing fabric, strengthening the rear spars, and maintaining a watch in the pilot's seat. His second problem, which had also been recognized by the searching ships, was the danger that they might pass between the islands and out to sea on the other side. If that happened they would surely die. The third problem, making a safe landing through the surf, would come later and only if they were successful in crossing the Kauai Channel.

Rodgers wrote in his report that he was apprehensive that they might repeat the tragic history of the *Saginaw*'s lifeboat. After making Kauai from Ocean Island, a distance of over 1,200 miles, the boat attempted to land at night on the north shore of Kauai. While coming through the surf the boat upset and all the crew were drowned except one man. Rodgers knew that in their weakened condition the possibility that he and his men would suffer a similar fate was very real.

Just before sunrise on 8 September, the *Langley* and *Reno* were plowing north toward their new search area. Suddenly a lookout reported flares bearing 160 degrees. The sighting was immediately confirmed by three officers on the bridge. The *Reno* and *Langley* swung around and increased speed to investigate. They searched an area nearly twenty miles long before calling off the search. It was now daylight and the ships were fifteen miles north of Kahului. The original course was resumed and another false alarm was chalked up.[6]

At 1100, the *Langley* and *Reno* started searching in their assigned area. Employing the same method they had used on 6–7 September, they worked three hours covering 800 square miles directly windward of Oahu. After recovering their aircraft the two ships steamed for three hours to the west, arriving at the next search area at 1700. Aircraft were again launched and the search continued for two more hours until the day's operations were stopped at 1900—one hour early.

Curtailing the day's search by one hour was a fateful decision. On the last sweep the *Langley*'s planes came very close to the *PN9–1*. Had they stayed up the remaining hour, they would undoubtedly have found the seaplane. However, after the planes were aboard, one was found to have a broken air pressure line. The pilot was unaware of this, but had he not landed when he did the *Langley* would have lost a plane and maybe a pilot.[7]

There is no doubt that these planes were close to the *PN9–1* on the evening of 8 September. In a postflight interview, Stantz stated that on that day he heard an airplane using the call sign assigned to the *PN9–1*. "At first I thought I was dreaming," he said.

But something else was taking place that Stantz did not hear about. At 2045 the commander of Submarine Division Nine reported that, in compliance with orders, his submarines were on line between Kaena Point on Oahu and Kahala Point on Kauai. Among the boats, which were spaced six-and-a-half miles apart, was the *R–4* commanded by Lieutenant Donald Osborn, Jr.[8]

At 0900 on 9 September Oahu was sighted. Though the *PN9–1* was still about fifty miles offshore, the island was clearly visible. Despite having been without water for over twenty-four hours, the land that seemed so close raised their flagging spirits.

Rodgers and Connell had still said nothing to the others about changing course away from Oahu. But Rodgers's sights, taken that morning after the island had come into view, showed that the time to make the course change had come. The men were assembled and told the decision; the news was not well received.

The decision to make the course change had been made at the last possible moment. Had the course been changed the previous evening the danger of missing Kauai would have been less. But because there had been a slim chance that the *PN9–1* could reach Oahu, Rodgers felt that he owed it to his crew to make every effort to reach the island. Only after his morning sights had shown that an attempt to reach Oahu would fail did Rodgers order the course change.

Pope was visibly shaken by the announcement. Connell said that after the course change Pope kept looking back at Oahu "as if he were losing his last friend and hope was gone." Pope could not reconcile sailing away from an island they could see in favor of one that was still out of sight.

Rodgers tried to explain to Pope why the course change had to be made. The *PN9–1*'s position relative to the island, and the direction of the wind and current, meant that the seaplane would be swept down the Kauai Channel and beyond the islands. Pope finally accepted the decision, but he did not like it.

Even with the course change the danger of being carried down the Kauai Channel and out to sea was not over. There were three critical factors upon which success depended; navigation, the lee boards, and the direction of the wind. Failure of any one of these three factors would mean disaster.

Navigation offered the least problem and the only danger from the lee boards was that they might fall off. This possibility was insignificant, however, due to the men's vigilance. The real danger was that the wind might shift to a position more forward of the plane as they crossed the Kauai Channel. A shift in the other direction—more aft of the plane—would have been a blessing but was too remote a possibility to even consider.

Shortly after changing course, a large black cloud was sighted ahead and preparations were made to catch water should the cloud pass over them. They took in their sails, draping them over the hull and forming pockets for the water to gather in. This time they were careful that the coated side of the fabric was up so that the water would not be absorbed by the fabric. They had just finished when the rain started. Water poured down in torrents and they all stood with their heads back and mouths open wide. Water ran in streams off the wings and hull, puddling in the pockets and depressions formed in the sails. The men scooped water from these canvas pools with their hands as fast as it gathered. For forty minutes the rain pounded down and then quit as abruptly as it had started. During that forty minutes, however, the men had collected three quarts of water.

After the rain stopped they licked the wet fabric and the metal hull trying to get every drop. Rodgers commented to Bowlin that often the cheapest things in life were the most valuable. Bowlin agreed but offered that at the moment water was not cheap.

The rain squall probably saved their lives. At the time Rodgers doubted that they could have lasted much longer. Bowlin said the same thing. "This I believe was the crucial point in the adventure for me . . . I doubt if any of us could have held out much longer without it." The fact that the water was impregnated with aluminum paint and dope, which made it taste awful, did not deter them at all. Within fifteen minutes after the squall the physical condition of everyone had improved dramatically.

Among the five men, Stantz showed the most dramatic recovery. Prolonged motion sickness accompanied by vomiting and lack of water had dehydrated him badly. His poor physical state had sapped his will to survive, which made his condition even more serious. Had the rain squall not passed over them when it did, Stantz might have died. But the water revived him and the realization that they were close to land boosted his sagging spirits. Though he was still very weak, Stantz was out of immediate danger.

At 1000 Rodgers saw two land planes searching along the north shore of Oahu. They were the *Langley*'s. Since early that morning, accompanied by the *Aroostook* and *Reno*, the carrier had been working the area north and east of Oahu. Part of the search area touched on the track down which the *PN9–1* was sailing. What Rodgers saw was the first two-plane element sent up that morning. The planes' search pattern brought them within fifteen miles of the drifting—now sailing—*PN9–1*.[9]

While the airmen aboard the *PN9–1* watched the *Langley*'s searching planes, things were happening on shore which added to the growing opinion that Rodgers and his men were dead. A Hawaiian walking along a beach about ten miles south of Hilo found two Navy life jackets. He left the jackets where they were and hurried to report the find. The two life jackets caused a great deal of excitement and a foot search was conducted for several miles along the beach on which the jackets had been found.[10]

The *Whippoorwill* and USS *Seagull* went to the area and searched the waters for wreckage or bodies. The *Hilo Tribune*, having heard of the find, offered "suitable rewards" to anyone picking up a part of the plane. The newspaper also organized a search along the south coast of Hawaii.[11]

Throughout the day, on 9 September, Oahu remained clearly visible from the drifting plane, a constant torment to Pope. The rest of the crew, having more easily accepted the decision to go on, were now straining to catch sight of Kauai. The fact that they now had a definite goal helped raise morale. But after dark they began to feel increasingly uneasy about the fact that they had to make Kauai or perish. Connell was more aware of their situation's effect on Rodgers than upon himself:

> The Commander did considerable worrying while navigating that night. On our trip across the channel toward Kauai the wind was such that if it changed only a few degrees we could not make land. The Commander took sights practically all night.

Pope was more aware of his own feelings:

> That night I did not try to go to sleep at all. Lieutenant Connell woke up and wanted to relieve me at the wheel, but I told

> him he could go ahead and sleep. I knew I could not sleep,
> even if I tried, until we had sighted Kauai. I stayed at the
> wheel most of the night, Rodgers relieved me once.

Bowlin also felt the effects of the "do or die" situation. "These
were trying moments as we waited for the time when a position
would be obtained where it would be impossible for us to miss
the island," he said.

Rodgers later admitted his anxiety during the night crossing
of the Kauai Channel. "It was a rather hard night for me, because
I had made the decision to go on and the responsibility was mine
for getting over to the island of Kauai." There was something
else about which the commander was worried. "Having failed
in the original plan," as he said, he was concerned over the
possibility of being court martialed.

After eight days at sea with little or no water, they now
enjoyed a surfeit of it. Throughout the night rain squalls passed
over them, the clouds obscuring the horizon and blotting out the
moon. At 2400 Rodgers called Connell forward to the navigator's
cockpit. The commander was obviously worried. Connell recalled the meeting clearly:

> About midnight he called me and I went forward and looked at
> the chart to see the position. The sight he had just taken was

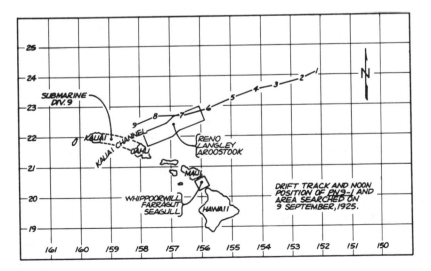

evidently in error, due to the fact that he had a very poor horizon, as the moon was partially obscured. This showed that we were losing latitude and would miss Kauai. I worried a lot in the next half hour, until later sights showed me we would just be able to make it if the wind held, by tacking the full amount possible with the improvised lee boards.

Shortly after midnight lights were seen on the clouds near the horizon and were assumed to be a destroyer's searchlights. Connell, previously unflappable, grabbed the flare gun and scrambled up onto the upper wing. He was firing as fast as he could load and pull the trigger when Rodgers told him to stop. The ships were too far away, and Rodgers wanted flares on hand in case a ship did come close enough.

For the remainder of the night most of the crew stayed awake. Stantz was the exception. The rain had definitely helped him but he was still very weak and had almost no energy. His condition weighed heavily on the others who believed that if they did not get help soon Stantz would die.

Until shortly after midnight they maintained a searchlight watch, and though they frequently saw what they thought were lights nothing came of them. After a time no more lights were seen and the crew went to sleep. Pope, who spent most of the night in the pilot's seat, summed up the general feeling:

> We continued at two-and-half knots. It was the most lonesome night of the whole journey, as it was the darkest night we had. It was the bluest too, for we knew our fate depended on the next day. We decided that if we missed Kauai we were lost, because no ships would search that side of the island.

At sunrise on 10 September the crew was anxiously straining to catch some sign of Kauai through the heavy rain squalls that obscured the island. During the tense night they had become increasingly worried. At 0900, however, they saw their goal through a momentary break in the weather. Kauai was directly ahead of them.

Since daybreak the search around the islands had been concentrated around Maui, Oahu, and Kauai. The *Langley*, with her escorts, was working much the same area as she had on the ninth. But the base course of this group extended the search

south and east of the *PN9–1*'s position. The *Langley* and her
escorts were now working behind the plane.[12]

The main hope for rescue came from the submarine scouting
line which ran between Point Kaena on Oahu and Point Kahala
on Kauai. The north end of this line lay astride the *PN9–1*'s
path. The submarines, having arrived on the scouting line at
1800 on the eighth, had retired down the Kauai Channel during
darkness. In the morning they reversed their course and worked
their way back up the channel, regaining the original line by
1800 on the ninth. That night the process was repeated. This
tide-like movement was intended to insure that the plane did not
drift down the Kauai Channel and get behind the submarine
line.[13]

By 1400 the men knew they were not going to be blown
past the island. Their fears over, they expressed their feeling by
back-slapping and compliments to Rodgers on his excellent navigation. Pope recalled the moment more clearly than the others:

> The island suddenly loomed up as if we were right on top of it.
> Everybody was so happy we almost forgot we were so weak
> and started moving around again. We complimented the Com-
> mander's good navigation, telling him we owed our lives to
> him. All he did was smile.

Revived by the sight of the island, they began to plan how
they would close on it and anchor. Several of them expected to
reach shore almost immediately. "Everyone started moving
around just as if we were bringing the ship into port," Pope told
reporters later. Rodgers knew, however, that getting ashore was
not going to be easy.

When Rodgers had decided to go to Kauai his intention was
to make the Ahukini Landing in Hanamaula Bay. He had two
reasons for choosing to land there. The harbor opened directly
in the direction of the trade wind, and a harbor master with a
motorboat was always on duty. To reach this goal he had worked
the plane to a point directly to windward of the harbor entrance.

They were now twenty miles offshore and Rodgers cor-
rectly estimated that their drift would bring them to the island
after dark. Thoroughly familiar with the island's shoreline, he
knew that the reefs and heavy swells made any landing danger-

ous. Rodgers had no intention of being wrecked after having safely sailed the plane 450 miles. A day landing would be hazardous enough; a night landing would be suicide. The only alternative was to stay out another night.

The decision was a blow to the crew. Rodgers tried to ease their disappointment by explaining the dangers involved. Connell summed up their feelings:

> The Commander, however, explained that it would be very dangerous to drift into the shoals and surf along Kauai that night. He explained that there were only two harbors where heavy surf would not be encountered. None of us had really realized this danger. We were just glad to see land, to get near it. I think we would have been tickled to death to drift onto the shore right then, though it might have been fatal, for we were too weak to swim through the surf.

The decision having been made, the next step was to take in the sails and rig a sea anchor with which to hold the plane off the island. The sea anchor was to be made from one of the fuel tanks; but first the tank had to be taken out of the hull. This was no small job. The fuel tanks had been built into the plane before the hull was completed, and the tank they intended to use was too big to be brought out through a cockpit opening. The only solution was to cut a hole in the top of the hull big enough to get the tank through. Inadequate tools and physical exhaustion made the job a major undertaking.

When the tank was out they planned to cut away one side, much like a sardine can, and punch holes in the opposite side. Then, after rigging a bridal, the tank would be towed behind the plane with the open side forward. The resulting drag would reduce their speed to nearly zero.

Because all the regular ground tackle had been left in San Francisco to save weight, they had to rig something to use as an anchor when the plane finally reached the harbor. A makeshift anchor was rigged using two starter batteries and a starter motor. The Aeromarine starter motor was the same one they had tried to use unsuccessfully to turn the radio generator. The starter motor was to fail in this second role as completely as in the first.

Assignments made, the crew went to work. Stantz, too weak to do any work, was put in the pilot's seat. He knew absolutely nothing about steering the plane, but his drunken meanderings helped slow the plane down. His inept handling of the controls also provided some much needed comic relief. Bowlin collected the storage batteries and starter motor to be used as an anchor, and pulled the control cables out of the hull to use as anchor cable. Commenting later on his efforts, Bowlin said, "I used the last ounce of strength I could muster to help get the anchor gear ready for landing."

Bowlin was not alone in feeling the effects of his labor. Pope and Connell had finally cleared away the metal skin over the gas tank and Pope dropped down into the hull:

> I felt so strong just being so near land that I rushed down and started to work on the tank. Suddenly I caved in. I almost collapsed. I called to Lieutenant Connell and all of us got around. That was the first we noticed how weak we really were.

The United States submarine *R–4* was moving up the Kauai Channel toward the scouting line which was still three hours and twenty minutes away. Under the command of Lieutenant Donald R. Osborn Jr., the *R–4* had been at sea for two weeks, the last nine days of which had been spent searching for the *PN9–1*.

At 1440 her second officer, Lieutenant (jg) W. S. Price, spotted an object on the port beam. He called Osborn and for the next thirty-four minutes the two officers watched the object. At 1514 they recognized it as an airplane and turned toward it.[14] As they neared the plane Osborn and Price could see men moving

The U.S. submarine *R–4*, commanded by Lieutenant Donald R. Osborn Jr., had been searching for nine days when she came upon the *PN9–1* fifteen miles off Kauai on 10 September 1925. U.S. Naval Institute photo.

around on the hull. Osborn recalled, "We hoped it was [the] *PN9–1*, but we were doubtful, because we thought no human could stand the strain of floating in a plane for more than nine days."[15] The boat increased speed and headed toward the plane to investigate.

The *PN9–1* was fifteen miles offshore. After the exhausting work of getting the sea anchor and improvised ground tackle ready the men were taking a break. Shortly, Rodgers suggested that they might be close enough to the island to attract help by signaling. The idea was received enthusiastically. Connell climbed atop the upper wing and began waving a piece of wing fabric back and forth. Rodgers and the others built a fire in a bucket. As they were building the fire Rodgers commented to the others, "It would be just like one of those guys to turn up now, just when we're about to make port."

A column of oily black smoke rose from the bucket while Connell waved his fabric flag and the others watched for some sign of recognition from land. Bowlin turned around for some reason and looked away from the island. He saw a submarine.

At first what he saw did not register because he was not looking for a ship any more. Suddenly he realized what he was seeing. His excited shout, "There's a submarine back of us," caught everybody's attention. Pope saw the boat coming toward them "four bells and a jingle." As the submarine rushed toward them the whole crew became excited. They were saved. There would not be another night on the plane after all.

At 1545 the *R–4* was alongside the plane. The first things the airmen wanted were water, food, and cigarettes. A heaving line was passed over and the supplies started across. During this activity, Rodgers and Osborn discussed the next step—towing. Osborn said he was going to tow them to Nawiliwili and asked if they wanted to come aboard the *R–4*. Rodgers declined the offer saying that they would complete the trip in the plane.[16]

After being out two weeks the submarine was not overly stocked with food. A five-gallon can of water was passed across along with some canned peaches, a package of bread, some sausages, and cigarettes. The delivery was to have included a pot of coffee, but the *R–4*'s cook had been so excited that he simply

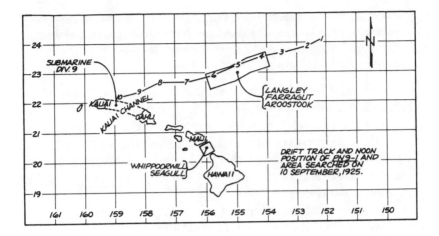

put the ground coffee in the bucket. That did not bother the airmen—the water was the first thing they wanted.[17]

While the towing gear was being arranged, the men took in the sails and secured the loose gear. They ate the canned peaches as they worked and were soon asking for more. By now the R-4 was only thirty feet away and the canned peaches were simply tossed across.

As the R-4 maneuvered to pick up the tow the fliers repeatedly expressed concern that the submarine would hit their plane. Osborn recalled several months later, "The fliers were worried for their plane and thought we would injure it in coming so close." The aviators were right. The R-4 struck and slightly damaged the leading edge of the starboard lower wing. Other than this minor incident, a pale reflection of the PN9-3's bout with the William Jones, the tow was picked up without problems.[18]

At 1600 the R-4 headed for Nawiliwili fifteen miles away with the PN9-1 in tow. During the trip Osborn made repeated offers to Rodgers to bring the men aboard. The offers were refused. For the next four hours the airmen relaxed and tried their first meal in several days. Connell described it:

After we were started we decided to have a much needed repast. We drank the water first. The Commander suggested that we put aluminum paint in it so it would taste natural. Then we opened cans of peaches, located a spoon and a granite cup and took turns devouring the peaches. Never have I tasted anything so good in my life. We did not dare try the sausage, for our stomachs would not stand heavy food.

They also talked about what they wanted most to eat. Pope wanted buttered toast, soft-boiled eggs, coffee, and a cigarette. Stantz wanted candy. Some of the men were concerned that they might have to spend the night aboard the submarine and Pope asked Rodgers about that. The commander had an immediate, positive answer, "I should say not. We'll go to a hotel and have a good meal."

At 1700, with the plane safely under tow, Lieutenant Osborn sent a message to Pearl Harbor that many had given up any hope of ever hearing: "Plane Prep Negative nine dash one located by Rodger Four, fifteen miles northeast of Nawiliwili. Personnel safe. Am towing same to Nawiliwili." The fleet now knew that the *PN9–1* had been found.

When the *R–4* and the *PN9–1* arrived at the entrance of the poorly lighted harbor the men saw the dangers about which Rodgers had been talking. The swells were high and the surf

The *PN9–1* in Nawiliwili Harbor 11 September 1925. One of the lee boards made from the metal flooring is hanging below the starboard wing. The damage done to the lower starboard wing when the *R–4* backed into it can also be seen. The canvas draped over the pilot's cockpit is one of the sails which had been made from the lower wing fabric. U.S. Navy photo.

was very heavy. Connell spoke for them all, "We could hear the surf pounding on the reefs and we realized that to have drifted in at night would have been fatal to the plane and might easily have resulted in loss of life."

Rodgers, in a press statement made several days later, described the last adventure with these words, "The most exciting part of the whole journey was getting the plane anchored safely in the harbor of Nawiliwili." In his official report he said, "We reached the harbor of Nawiliwili after dark and our troubles began."

Inside the breakwater there was a large reef which prevented the submarine from entering the harbor. The *R–4* slowly nosed into the harbor entrance, maneuvering to avoid the reef. The *PN9–1* with the wind dead astern, began to creep up on the submarine. The tow line dipped lower in the water as the strain decreased. The *R–4*'s engines went astern and the gap between the *R–4* and *PN9–1* quickly narrowed. The tow line sagged. As the submarine slowly backed away from the reef she passed over the tow line. In an instant the line was wrapped around the *R–4*'s propellers.

Immediately an anchor was put down and chain paid out as the *R–4*'s momentum continued to carry her astern. The chain was snubbed to set the anchor and as the anchor dug in the load on the chain increased. Suddenly the chain snapped. Frantic activity followed during which a new anchor was put down and swimmers were sent over the side to free the propellers. About this time, Osborn wanted to rid himself of the airplane while he looked after his own problems. Rodgers agreed, but said he could not cast off until he had an anchor. Osborn sent a swimmer across to the plane with a line and a fifty-pound mushroom anchor was hauled across. When the anchor was aboard the *PN9–1*, the tow lines were cast off. The *PN9–1* was on her own again.[19]

The seaplane drifted away from the submarine while the crew bent a line to the anchor. As soon as the ground tackle was ready, Rodgers had the anchor dropped over the side and let out as much scope as he had line available. The *PN9–1* was windward of the reef and Rodgers's frequent checks soon showed that the anchor was dragging.[20]

The *Tanager* arrived at 2100 and Stantz signaled that they were dragging and needed a heavier anchor. The *Tanager*'s sailing launch was lowered and a 100-pound anchor was put aboard. But instead of going directly to the plane the sailing launch steered for the *R–4*.

In the meantime the arrival of the submarine and the plane had attracted a large crowd on the beach and several small boats had put off from the shore to have a closer look. Among them was a four-oared pulling boat which rowed over to the submarine and joined the *Tanager*'s sailing launch. The crew of the sailing launch did not think that they could maneuver in close to the plane because of their mast and boom. They asked the Hawaiians in the pulling boat to take the anchor to the plane. The civilians were only too happy to help. The anchor was transferred to their boat and they set off for the *PN9–1*.

As the pulling boat rowed toward the plane a powerboat passed and got to the *PN9–1* first. Rodgers saw his chance to keep his plane off the reef and get to a better anchorage inside the harbor. He asked the two men in the powerboat if they would tow the plane farther into the harbor. The powerboaters eagerly agreed and passed a line to Rodgers.

Rodgers was taking a turn around the bow cleat when the boat owner suddenly realized that his boat was drifting onto the reef. In panic he slammed the throttle forward, causing the boat to surge ahead jerking the line tight. The line curled around Rodger's left hand and snapped his middle finger.

But the pain in his hand was momentarily forgotten when Rodgers saw they were being dragged directly toward the reef. In his panic, the boat owner was headed across the reef jerking the *PN9–1* behind him. Everyone in the plane held their breath but the *PN9–1* did not touch as both boat and plane shot across the sharp coral.

As the plane entered the quiet water on the other side, Rodgers tried to cast off the tow line with his one good hand. He was unable to because the line was still under load. There was not even time to signal the boat owner to stop. Still running at full speed, the motorboat whipped about and charged at the reef a second time. The *PN9–1* bounced along behind as her horrified skipper gritted his teeth and waited for the crash.

The five crewmen on Kauai on 11 September 1925. L to R: Stantz, Bowlin, Rodgers, Connell, and Pope. Rodgers's left hand is heavily bandaged as a result of the broken finger he suffered during the tow into the harbor. National Archives photo 80–G–459809.

On the second crossing the plane touched. The noise of metal scraping across coral was awful. The sound was as though her whole bottom had opened up. Rodgers felt sick. The others were in a state of shock. Attempts were now made to get the fool in the powerboat to wake up and stop. Rodgers would rather take his chances outside the reef than submit to any more such towing. The effort to stop the boat was wasted. The five fliers nearly had a group coronary when they realized that the imbecile in the boat was headed back toward the reef for a third time.

Bowlin and Pope had already made a quick check and found that the hull was still tight. Now both rushed forward with their knives to cut the towline before the plane got to the reef again. They were too late. Everyone hung on and prayed as the *PN9–1* made her third crossing behind the powerboat. Nothing touched. As soon as the plane was inside the reef and in calm water, Bowlin severed the line with his knife. The *PN9–1* slowed and turned her bow into the wind. She was safe. They threw their storage battery and starter motor anchor over the side to check their drift toward the beach, but the plane was still drifting when the four-oared pulling boat finally caught up and came along side. The pulling boat's crew had the *Tanager*'s 100-pound anchor and knew where there was good holding ground. The airmen took the anchor aboard and, reassured by the leisurely pace of the pulling boat, allowed the rowers to tow them to a safe anchorage. At 2000, two hours and a broken finger after their arrival, the *PN9–1* was safely anchored. Another hour was spent securing the plane and checking to be sure she was not dragging her anchor. At 2300 the five airmen went ashore to a hero's welcome.

Epilogue

In his postflight report, Lieutenant Commander Strong bitterly described the project as a "flat failure." His judgement was not entirely accurate. The attempt to fly nonstop to Hawaii had failed largely because the attempt was premature. The PN9, though an exceptional airplane, had only a marginal capacity for making the flight. That fact was obvious from the start, and for that reason the trade winds had been critical. It was not until 1934 that the Navy had a flying boat with sufficient range to reach Hawaii from the west coast, and another year would pass before regularly scheduled civilian flights were made between the two points.

In addition to having failed to complete the flight, the *PN9–1* had also failed to locate the *Aroostook*, the fault of bad radio bearings from the ship. There is no official explanation for the bad bearings, but it would seem reasonable to assume that equipment malfunction and operator error were responsible.

There is also the question of why the *Aroostook* failed to act on the radio bearings sent by the *Farragut*. The bearings taken by the destroyer at 1520 and 1533 were accurate and in agreement with the last visual bearing taken at 1314. Official records show that the *Farragut*'s radio bearings were sent to the *Aroostook* but were not acknowledged by the tender.[1]

The radio logs of both ships show that the *Farragut* was calling the *Aroostook* at those times. But the *Aroostook*'s radio log does not record any radio bearings having been received from the destroyer. The entries merely state, "*Farragut* calling *Aroostook*." In his official report the *Aroostook*'s captain said that there was a great deal of atmospheric and commercial interference during the critical period. This interference may have covered the final part of the *Farragut*'s transmission which contained the radio bearings.[2]

133

There was a third failure associated with the attempt—the failure of the guardships to quickly locate the *PN9–1*. The fault did not rest entirely with the *Aroostook*'s bad radio bearings. Contributing to the confusion was the fact that Rodgers did not keep the *Aroostook* informed about the *PN9–1*'s course and estimated position.[3] Had he done that, the discrepancy between the *PN9–1*'s position as shown by the radio bearings and the plane's position according to Rodgers's DR would have been obvious from the start. The problem could thus have been corrected, and the *PN9–1* would probably have found the *Aroostook*.

Beyond the immediate and publicly announced goal of making a nonstop flight to Hawaii, there was the *real* goal of preventing naval aviation from being taken from the fleet and incorporated into an independent air force. The planes certainly failed to accomplish the nonstop flight. The failure, accompanied by the negative publicity and in conjunction with the *Shenandoah*'s loss, seemed initially to have hurt the Navy's cause and to have advanced General Mitchell's. Mitchell thought so too, and his

The USS *Pelican* underway to Pearl Harbor with the *PN9–1* on the fantail. National Archives photo 80–G–179339.

5 September statement was calculated to capitalize on the Navy's dual misfortune.

In fact, and unintentionally, the reverse was true. The *PN9–1*'s apparent loss, the *Shenandoah*'s destruction, and Mitchell's outburst served to focus the nation's attention on the sad state of American aviation. The issues of whether or not to have an independent air force, and the government's relationship to the aviation industry, were thus brought to a head.

Had the *PN9–1* succeeded in reaching Hawaii as planned, Mitchell would have had only the *Shenandoah* crash to point to. One disaster offset by a dramatic success would probably have greatly diminished the impact of Mitchell's explosive statement— if he would have made such a statement at all. Had that been the case, the struggle between the independent air force backers and the Navy's Bureau of Aeronautics might have gone on for many more years without a decision. A protracted debate would have continued to retard America's aviation development. The attendant uncertainty in the private and military sectors would have enhanced Mitchell's argument for an independent air force.

But the *PN9–1* did disappear, the *Shenandoah* did crash, and Mitchell did make his vituperative attack upon both the Army and Navy high commands. Mitchell's subsequent court martial was merely a side result of these events. The important result was that President Coolidge appointed almost immediately a board to report on "the best means of developing and applying aircraft in national defense."[4] In effect, naval aviation was to have its day in court, and win.

The board, headed by Dwight W. Morrow, first met on 17 September 1925—just seven days after the *PN9–1* had been found and eleven days after Mitchell's statement had been splashed across the front pages of the nation's newspapers. The hearings lasted four weeks, during which time ninety-nine witnesses were called. The witnesses included Army and Navy fliers, senior military officers, and representatives of the aviation industry and government.

Out of the hearings came a lengthy report which, among other things, recommended against the establishment of a British style Air Ministry responsible for all aviation matters. The board

AP rushed to, or telephoned, the homes of the crew members. When Rodgers's brother, Robert, heard the news over the telephone he said, "Will you please read that again?" In Richmond, Indiana, Bowlin's aunt, Mrs E. E. Orr, responded to the news with "Oh thank God. My prayers are answered!" Mrs. Stantz, the radioman's wife, told AP reporters, "Never once during the search for Otis have I lost confidence that he would be found well and alive, but before the start of the flight I felt that some mishap would befall the plane." Stantz's five-year-old son exclaimed, "Oh, they've found my daddy." In Jackson, Tennessee, Pope's sister, Estella, was so overcome with emotion that she asked the AP reporter to tell the details to her friend, Miss Maude Gilbert.[6]

In San Francisco, newspaper extras were issued and the news was flashed on every theater screen in town while "wild applause swept the theater." The showmanship so common to politics and so recently given full reign during California's Diamond Jubilee had not been fully exhausted by San Francisco's politicians. They immediately insisted that the heroes be returned to San Francisco—aboard none other, of course, than the battleship USS *California*.[7]

The *PN9–1* crew, however, was returned to San Francisco aboard the battleship USS *Idaho*. After several public appearances including luncheons and dinners, the men were sent off on leave. Commander Rodgers, who had been appointed Admiral Moffett's assistant in the Bureau of Aeronautics, made several radio addresses intended to build support for naval aviation.

Because of the publicity value of a flight over Honolulu, Rodgers's flagship was speedily repaired. From Nawiliwili, the plane was rushed to Pearl Harbor where every available man was put to work rebuilding her. On 19 September, just six days after she had entered the hanger, the *PN9–1* was again airborne. But by the end of October 1925 the public's interest in the *PN9–1* had waned, and the epic flight was quickly forgotten.

The *PN9–3*, last seen floating belly up in San Francisco Bay, was also rebuilt. After being fished out of the water, she was taken to Mare Island and completely disassembled. There

22 September 1925. The *PN9–1* was back in the air. National Archives photo 80–G–465336.

was, however, no urgency in completing her repairs. Some of the work was done at Mare Island, more was done at NAF, Philadelphia, and the airplane was finally reassembled in San Diego.

In 1926 both PN9's became part of an experimental scouting squadron at North Island, San Diego, but their careers were short. The *PN9–3* was destroyed during a storm on 13 March 1927 while being transported aboard the USS *West Virginia*. The *PN9–1* was lost nineteen days later on a routine training flight.[8]

The *PB1* never did get a shot at the transpacific flight. After several trouble-filled test flights in San Francisco the plane was returned to the Boeing factory in Seattle. In 1928 Boeing reengined the plane with Pratt and Whitney R–1960 "Hornet" radial, air-cooled engines and changed the designation to XPB–2. But by that time, due to advancements in aviation technology, the airplane was a dinosaur by any name, and in 1932 she was scrapped.[9]

Bowlin and Connell survived into the 1960's. Bowlin was later commissioned and retired from the Navy as a lieutenant commander. Connell remained active in naval aviation until his retirement in 1947. During his career he went on to establish several world records in seaplanes for distance, speed, and altitude. In August 1927 he kept a Packard-powered PN–10 in the air for twenty hours and forty-five minutes—less time than the *PN9–1* had been airborne during her Pacific flight.

Pope and Stantz both remained in the Navy but drifted out of the limelight after 1927. Pope was involved in the PN series development program at NAF, and accompanied Connell on at least one of Connell's record-setting flights.

Commander Strong resigned from the the Navy in 1939 and died in Morrisville, Pennsylvania, in 1961. Ralph E. Davison, described by Admiral Moffet as "the most level headed in the bunch,"[10] commanded Task Force 78 during the landings at Hollandia in April 1944.

Donald Osborn, Jr., reached the rank of captain and retired in 1949, after a long and successful Navy career. His boat, the *R–4*, lasted nearly as long, serving continuously until she was struck from the Navy list in 1945 and scrapped.

What happened to the ships that guarded the route, and the *Gannet* which had been the service vessel in San Francisco? The *Aroostook* enjoyed a long career, the *Gannett*, *Tanager*, and *Langley* died violently during World War II, and between 1930 and 1932, all the destroyers suffered an ignominious end under the breaker's hammer in accordance with the 1930 London Naval Treaty.

Tragic deaths awaited Admiral Moffett and Commander Rodgers. Moffett died in the crash of the airship *Akron* on 4 April 1933. Commander Rodgers died on 27 August 1926— almost one year exactly after he had set out for Hawaii—in a strange aircraft accident.[11]

At 1040 on 27 August Commander Rodgers took off from Anacostia NAS in a Vought VE–9, a two-place, single-engine, biplane equipped with wheels. Aboard the VE–9 in the aft cockpit was Aviation Machinist's Mate Samuel J. Schultz. Their destination was NAF, Philadelphia, where Rodgers was to inspect the latest model PN. After a short stop in Aberdeen, Maryland, Rodgers flew on, arriving over NAF at 1330.

Aviation Rigger, 2nd class, Paul Wirick was sitting in front of a hanger. He watched the small biplane circle the field in a "rather close turn" and then suddenly drop in a "very quick spin" from an altitude of about 150 feet. The VE–9 came down vertically, making two complete revolutions, and crashed into the Delaware River.

The plane crashed 100 yards offshore, nose down in four feet of water. Rescue efforts were started at once by men who had either waded out to the crash or arrived in boats. Schultz was quickly removed from the after cockpit and rushed ashore. Rodgers was trapped in the wreckage, his shattered leg "all twisted amongst the floor boards and the firewall." He also had suffered massive internal injuries.

For over an hour the men worked to free Rodgers, whose condition was rapidly deteriorating. As the rescue operations went on, a situation developed right out of a Hollywood script. At the time, all of the former *PN9–1*'s crew were stationed at NAF, where they were involved in further development of the PN type. One by one, they now began showing up at the accident, although none of them knew that the trapped, dying pilot was Rodgers. The discovery that it was their former captain was a shocking, emotional affair for each one.

Rodgers, who had regained consciousness, recognized and spoke to each of his ex-crewmen. His conversation was generally rational except for a strange statement that he made repeatedly to each crewman, "Tell them it wasn't my eyes."

Rodgers was at last freed from the tangled wreckage and taken ashore by boat. An ambulance was waiting which rushed him the short distance to the base hospital. By then Rodgers was too far gone to save. Even as the doctors were undressing him, Rodgers's color was becoming more dusky. At 1700 on 27 August 1926 Commander John Rodgers died.

There remains only an historical postscript. On 28 June 1927 an Army Fokker tri-motor left Oakland, California, en route to Hawaii. Twenty-five hours and forty minutes later the plane landed at Wheeler Field. The pilot, Lieutenant Albert F. Hegenberger, had succeeded where Rodgers had failed. But Hegenberger's accomplishment had little effect on the airpower issue, whereas Rodgers's epic adventure had helped decide the issue two years earlier. Though Rodgers and his crew failed to fly to Hawaii, their attempt had proven to be a "successful" failure.

Appendix

Technical Details of the PN9's and PB-1

PN-9

Manufacturers: Naval Aircraft Factory, June 1924–April 1925.

Designation: PN8 (June 1924–March 1925) PN9 (March 1925-) Numbers A–6799 and A–6878. The bureau numbers assigned to the PN8's in June 1924 were carried through to the PN9's after the redesignation in March 1925.

Engines: 2; Packard 1A–1500, water-cooled, V–8, 525 hp.

Propellers: NAF, 2-blade wood with metal-clad tips and edges, 13′ dia.

Wings: Model USA–27. Composite construction, wood and metal frame covered with dope-treated fabric. Upper wing span 72′ 10″; lower wing span 67′ 2″; total wing area 1,217 sq. ft.

Hull: Steel frame covered with Duralumin.

Tail: Composite construction as wings.

Fuel Tanks: Nine mounted in the hull, total capacity: *PN9–1* 1,270 gal., *PN9–3* 1,252 gal. Fifty to 80 gal. carried in 5 gal. cans. Thirty gal. gravity fuel tanks in center upper wing, filled from main tanks.

Performance: Speed: cruising 70 knots, max. 114.5 knots; range: 1,800–1,900 nautical miles.

Crew: 5: 1 navigator, 2 pilots, 1 mechanic, 1 radioman.

Communications: A closeline type message trolly ran the length of the hull between the navigator and the radioman. A signal light system operated between the pilots' cockpit and the navigator. The engineer crawled forward to shout his message or deliver a hand-written note to the pilot or the navigator.

Comments: The PN–9 showed no adverse flight characteristics, and handled well on the water. An unattractive feature was the unadjustable rudder bar. The PN–9 was part of a development series which ended with PN–12. The experience gained with these few experimental flying boats eventually led to the development of the famous Catalina.

PB–1

Manufacturers: Boeing Company, 23 September 1924–5 August 1925.

Designation: Boeing Model 50, Navy PB–1 and XPB–2, Number A–6881.

Engines: 2; Packard 1A–2500, water-cooled V–8, 800 hp ea., August 1925.

Packard 3A–2500, same, August 1925–April 1928.

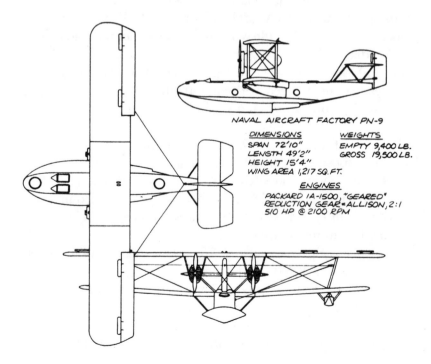

NAVAL AIRCRAFT FACTORY PN-9

DIMENSIONS
SPAN 72'10"
LENGTH 49'2"
HEIGHT 15'4"
WING AREA 1,217 SQ.FT.

WEIGHTS
EMPTY 9,400 LB.
GROSS 19,500 LB.

ENGINES
PACKARD 1A-1500, "GEARED"
REDUCTION GEAR = ALLISON, 2:1
510 HP @ 2100 RPM

Pratt & Whitney R–1690, air-cooled radial, 475 hp each, April
1928–October 1929.

Pratt & Whitney R–1860, same, 575 hp each, October 1929–June
1932.

Rolls Royce "H" water-cooled V- (additional information not
available) October 1932.

Propellers: Hamilton 4-blade wood with metal tips. Forward
12′8″ diameter, aft 11′0″ diameter. Subsequent propeller
changes were numerous and the radial engines had 3-blade
props.

Wings: Model "Clark-Y," developed at McCook Field. Composite construction, metal frame covered with dope-treated
fabric. Wing tips and leading edges wood. Span upper and
lower wings 87′6″, chord 11″. Total wing area 1,801 sq. ft.,
gap between wings 13′5″.

Hull: Composite construction, upper half laminated wood over
wood frames; lower half Duralumin skin over steel frames.

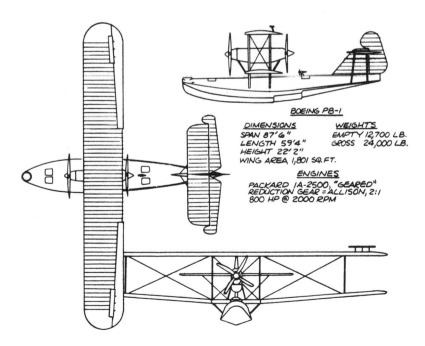

BOEING PB-1

DIMENSIONS
SPAN 87′6″
LENGTH 59′4″
HEIGHT 22′2″
WING AREA 1,801 SQ.FT.

WEIGHTS
EMPTY 12,700 LB.
GROSS 24,000 LB.

ENGINES
PACKARD 1A-2500, "GEARED"
REDUCTION GEAR = ALLISON, 2:1
800 HP @ 2000 RPM

Tail: Horizontal plane, dope-treated fabric over wood, vertical stabilizer and rudder, F–5L type, dope-treated fabric over wood.

Fuel Tanks: Six mounted in the hull amidships. Total capacity 1,812 gal.

Performance: Speed: cruising 80 knots, max. 125 knots; range: no endurance test was completed to determine her actual range. Several attempts were made, but engine failure forced the plane down each time. Estimated: 2,264 nautical miles in 1925, 2,630 nautical miles in 1928.

Crew: 5: 1 navigator, 2 pilots, 1 mechanic, 1 radioman.

Comments: The *PB–1* was never successful. She was used to test the feasibility of using various engines in tandem. Because of the tandem arrangement, the *PB–1* was extremely difficult to maneuver on the water. Depending upon the pilot's attitude, she was either a jewel or a dog to fly. Davison and Botta said she handled better than the PN–9s, but Strong said her controls were too heavy. In 1932 a pilot from NAF reported that she had "undesirable control characteristics" and she was "not considered a comfortable or enjoyable plane to fly." The *PB–1*, by then the *XPB–2*, was struck from the Navy list in November 1932.

Source Notes

An abbreviated form has been used when citing the two primary sources. Those sources are: Bureau of Aeronautics File Nr. A4–3 (7–1), Navy and Old Army Branch, National Archives, Washington, D.C. and The Rodgers Family Papers, Library of Congress, Washington, D.C.

The material found in the BURAERO file will be cited by the document title followed by A4–3 (7–1). Material found in The Rodgers Family Papers will be cited by the document title followed by RFP.

Introduction

1. Associated Press (AP) as reported in the *San Jose Mercury Herald*, 6 September 1925. AP carried the entire text of Mitchell's lengthy statement.

2. The documents describing the process that finally resulted in the project's approval, as well as the arguments for and against the early proposals, are too numerous to list. All found in A4–3 (7–1). Also see Aviation History Unit File Copy, "Rodgers' Flight to Hawaii." (Hereafter cited as "Rodgers Flight to Hawaii").

3. Lieutenant Commander J. H. Strong, "PB–1 Report on Preparations for the West Coast-Hawaii Flight and Endurance Tests in San Francisco Bay," 8 October 1925, Navy and Old Army Branch, RG 80. (Hereafter cited as Strong Report).

4. A detailed description of the Packard 1500 and 2500 engines is found in: Victor W. Page, *Modern Aviation Engines*, pp. 1437–1489.

5. The details of the test flight and problems which followed are taken from the following: Manager, NAF, "PN–9: Flights on," 20 April 1925; Manager, NAF, "PN–9: Preliminary report of endurance run on A6878," 5 May 1925; Chief Bureau of Aeronautics, "Report of PN–9 performance (A6878)," 16 June 1925; and Chief, Bureau of Aeronautics, "Model PN–9 Airplane," 5 June 1925. A4–3 (7–1).

6. Chief, Bureau of Aeronautics, "Airplane Flight West Coast of United States to Hawaiian Islands," 14 April 1925; Chief, Bureau of

Aeronautics, "Model of PN–9 Airplane," 5 June 1925; and Chief, Bureau of Aeronautics, "Report of PN–9 performance (A6878)," 16 June 1925. A4–3 (7–1).

7. Chief, Bureau of Aeronautics, "Model PN–9 Airplane," 5 June 1925; and Chief, Bureau of Aeronautics, "Report of PN–9 performance (A6878)," 16 June 1925. A4–3 (7–1).

San Diego, 18 June-22 August 1925

1. Chief, BURAERO, "Report of PN9 Performance," 16 June 1925; Chief, BURAERO, "Model PN9 Airplanes," 5 June 1925; and Mgr. NAF "PN9 Airplane A–6878," 26 May 1925. A4–3 (7–1).

2. See, for example, AP releases for 29 August 1925 and 2 September 1925.

3. CNO (Air), *U.S. Naval Aviation 1910–1970*, p. 6.

4. Actually, although Rodgers was not involved in aviation from 1912–1922, he was assigned to submarines only from 1916 to 1919. The point is that duty aboard one of the early submarines was a dubious sanctuary from the perils of aviation.

5. The information on the three aircrews comes from the *San Francisco Chronicle*, 30 August 1925 and AP as reported in the *San Jose Mercury Herald*, 31 August 1925.

6. *New York Times*, 21 September 1925.

7. *San Francisco Chronicle*, 21 July 1925.

8. *San Francisco Chronicle*, 22 July 1925; Thornwell Mullally, Telegram, 23 July 1925; and BURAERO, US Naval Message, 24 July 1925. A4–3 (7–1).

9. Strong Report.

10. "Rodgers' Flight to Hawaii."

11. Each airplane which was to take part in the flight was given a position number. Rodgers's PN9 became the *PN9–1*. The Boeing entry was the second airplane and Snody's PN9 was the third. Thus Snody's plane was the *PN9–3*, but the *PB1* never had her flight position number included in her designation. "Instructions, West Coast-Hawaii Seaplane Flight," 2 July 1925 (hereafter cited as "Instructions"). A4–3 (7–1).

12. *New York Times*, 21 September 1925.

13. *San Francisco Chronicle*, 21 July 1925.

14. Rodgers had good reason for having doubts. One of the suggested changes had been to use a new type of molybdenum side-electrode spark plug. Tests in San Diego showed that after a few hours running the plugs became heavily fouled with carbon, so badly that

they could not be used. Commander Rodgers, "Voyage of *PN9–1* Seaplane from San Francisco to Hawaii" 31 October 1925 (hereafter cited as the Rodgers Report). A4–3 (7–1).

15. Ibid.

16. When the *PN9–1* made her first test flight in San Diego on 28 July, her radiators leaked as badly as the *PN9–3*'s. *San Diego Union*, 24 July 1925; *San Francisco Chronicle*, 26 July 1925; *San Diego Union*, 29 July 1925; Rodgers Report; and Rodgers, Radiogram, 27 July 1925. A4–3 (7–1).

17. Lieutenant Arthur Gavin, "*PN9–3*, Training of crew and Attempted Flight to Hawaii" 30 September 1925 (hereafter cited as Gavin Report). A4–3 (7–1).

18. The details of the radiator crisis are found in the following documents: Aeronautics, US Naval Message, 27 July 1925; NAS San Diego, Radio Message Nr. 81223, 28 July; and NAS San Diego, Radio Message, Nr. 81224, 28 July 1925 (both messages are time-stamped 0400); West Coast-Hawaii Flight Unit Commander, Radiogram, Nr. 81801, 29 July 1925; Aeronautics, US Naval Message Nr. 68953, 29 July 1925; and Bureau of Aeronautics, US Naval Message Nr. 69215, 30 July 1925. A4–3 (7–1).

19. Some of the replies Moses gave Van Auken did not really address the issue. In reply to Van Auken's suggestion that the planes might not stay together after takeoff, Moses simply referred Van Auken to the official instructions, which stated that the planes were to remain together. In fact, the airplanes did not stay together after takeoff and soon lost sight of each other. Commander Aircraft Squadrons, Battle Fleet, "Questions submitted by Commanding Officer USS *Aroostook*," 28 July 1925. A4–3 (7–1).

20. In his report written on 8 October 1925, Strong placed the first flight on 5 August. But radio messages sent on 30 July said that the initial flight took place on 28 July. Subsequent requests for spare radiators and an engine for the *PB1* support the 28 July date. But there is no doubt that the *PB1* flew again on 5 August and burst a radiator. Strong Report.

21. The details of the frantic search for an engine and radiators are found in: West Coast-Hawaii Flight Unit Commander, Radio Message, 5 August 1925; Inspector of Engineering Material, Pittsburg, Pa., Letter, 1 August 1925; Aeronautics US Naval Message Nr. 69826, 1 August 1925; and Inspector Naval Aircraft at Seattle, Telegram Nr. 85343, 7 August 1925. A4–3 (7–1).

22. Strong Report.

23. *San Jose Mercury Herald*, 24 August 1925; and Rodgers Report.

San Francisco, 22–31 August 1925

1. According to hanger gossip, the *PB1* had nearly been battered to pieces by engine vibrations. Boeing was reportedly so alarmed about the *PB1*'s poor condition that they asked the NAF engineers to help correct the problem. The hanger gossip was exaggerated, but the report does give some idea of how serious the problems with the *PB1* were. This report is from *San Diego Union*, 27 August 1925.

2. *New York Times*, 21 September 1925; "Rodgers Flight to Hawaii;" and "Schedule of Operations-Period August 17–28th incl.," 15 August 1925, RFP.

3. Rodgers Report.

4. *San Francisco Chronicle*, 29 August 1925.

5. Lt. A. P. Snody, "Report on West Coast-Hawaii Flight (*PN9–3*)." 23 September 1925 (hereafter cited as Snody Report). A4–3 (7–1).

6. Gavin Report; Rodgers Report; and Associated Press as reported in *San Jose Mercury Herald*, 31 August 1925.

7. 30 August was not the first day since the fliers' arrival in San Francisco that the wind had howled. On 26 August the usual San Francisco August weather prompted a *San Diego Union* reporter to write: "It is no secret that the crews of the Hawaii flight planes wish devoutly that the start of the flight could be made from San Diego. San Francisco Bay this afternoon was a mass of white caps. The wind will hit the Hawaiian flight planes square on the nose when they come winging down from San Pablo Bay." *San Diego Union*, 27 August 1925; Snody Report; and Rodgers Report.

8. Rodgers Report.

9. Ibid; and *New York Times*, 21 September 1925.

10. The Navy officer who briefed the press representatives on the safety measures being taken must have had a strong sense of humor and a remarkably straight face. One AP reporter described one of the safety devices he had heard about: "A third safety device . . . is none other than the humble automobile inner tube, which makes a capital life preserver." The reporter did allow that there would be some difficulty in getting the tube inflated, especially in respect to time. He concluded: "Time is usually a most precious quantity in neutralizing the effects of the average airplane mishap." Associated Press as reported in the *San Jose Mercury Herald*, 30 August 1925; and Rodgers Report.

11. L. S. Howeth, *History of Communications-Electronics in the United States Navy*, pp. 278–279.

12. Rodgers Report.

13. The only account of the meeting is in Rodgers's postflight interview in *New York Times*, 21 September 1925.

14. Strong's disappointment was greater than Rodgers realized or wanted to admit. In commenting on the outcome of the meeting Strong said, "Coming after months of effort, the decision broke the morale of the crew and left us bitterly discouraged and disappointed. The wisdom of the decision will remain in doubt since the entire project ended in flat failure." Strong Report.

The Flight, 31 August–1 September 1925

1. *San Francisco Chronicle*, 1 September 1925.

2. Rodgers Report.

3. Ibid.

4. Rodgers Report; Snody Report; and Gavin Report.

5. In a postflight interview, Connell told a *New York Times* reporter that during the six-mile takeoff run he swore, "I'll break this thing or sink it or I'll get it off." *New York Times*, 23 September 1925.

6. Snody wrote in his report, "No trouble was experienced getting through the Golden Gate, though an Admiral Line steamship insisted on the right-of-way in the channel. This I readily granted, but it required a sharp change of course." Snody Report.

7. *New York Times*, 23 September 1925.

8. The actual distance along the flight path between San Francisco's Point Bonita and Kahului, Hawaii, was 2,036 nautical miles. The additional leg from Kahului to Honolulu brought the total air distance to about 2,100 nautical miles. Letter, no author given, Nr. AER–A–4–ERG/A4–3 (7–1) /804–21, 21 April 1926. A4–3 (7–1).

9. Captain Moses had arranged for "such submarines and vessels or other craft" based at Pearl Harbor to assist in the event that a search was necessary. Commander Flight Project, "Additional Plane Guard Vessels, West Coast-Hawaii Seaplane Flight," 11 July 1925; and "Supplemental Instructions for West Coast-Hawaii Flight," 5 August 1925. A4–3 (7–1).

10. Snody Report.

11. "Activity of USS *William Jones* (308) in connection with West Coast-Hawaii Flight-Report of," 15 September 1925 (hereafter cited as USS *William Jones*). A4–3 (7–1).

12. Snody had turned the controls over to Gavin after clearing the Golden Gate. Gavin had reduced the rpm so much that the engines actually did "cut-out." After that the minimum rpm was 1,900. Snody

Report. The conditions aboard the *PN9–1* are described in Rodgers Report.

13. The events regarding the *PN9–3* described here are taken from Snody Report and Gavin Report.

14. USS *William Jones;* USS *McCawley*, "Participation in the West Coast-Hawaii Airplane Flight-Report of," 2 October 1925 (hereafter cited as the USS *McCawley*). A4–3 (7–1); and Rodgers Report.

15. The station was NPW. Rodgers Report.

16. *San Francisco Chronicle*, 1 September 1925.

17. Ibid; and Associated Press as reported in the *San Jose Mercury Herald*, 1 September 1925.

18. USS *William Jones*.

19. Though the leeward position proved to be a tactical error in this case, this was one of the techniques recommended for picking up a downed seaplane. "Information for Merchant Ships, West Coast-Hawaii Non-Stop Seaplane Flight," undated. A4–3 (7–1).

20. USS *William Jones;* and Gavin Report.

21. USS *Corry*, "West Coast-Hawaii Flight-Plane Guard Ship for," 15 September 1925 (hereafter cited as USS *Corry*). A4–3 (7–1); and Rodgers Report.

22. USS *Meyer*, "Activity of USS *Meyer* on Duty in Connection with West Coast-Hawaiian Flight-Report on," 20 September 1925 (hereafter cited as USS *Meyer*). A4–3 (7–1); and Rodgers Report.

23. Rodgers Report.

24. The USS *Doyen*, "Detailed Report on Activities while on West Coast-Hawaiian non-stop flight duty," 12 September 1925 (hereafter cited as USS *Doyen*). A4–3 (7–1); and Rodgers Report.

25. On 1 September the *PN9–1* passed the *Doyen* at 0445, the *Langley* at 0730, and the *Reno* at 1030. The total time was 5 hours 45 minutes and the distance was 400 miles. USS *Doyen;* USS *Langley*, "West Coast-Hawaii Flight (1925); and USS *Reno*, "Report of Activities in Connection with West Coast-Hawaiian Airplane Flight," 1 October 1925 (hereafter cited as USS *Langley* and USS *Reno*). A4–3 (7–1).

26. Rodgers Report; and USS *Langley*.

27. USS *Reno*.

28. Rodgers Report.

29. Rodgers Report; and USS *Farragut*, Report, 18 September 1925 (hereafter cited as USS *Farragut*). A4–3 (7–1).

30. USS *Aroostook*. "Report of *Aroostook*," 11 September 1925 (hereafter cited as USS *Aroostook*). A4–3 (7–1).

31. The complete message was "Your position from Aroostook was 69 degrees at 1256. Ship on station Vice." The messages sent

between the *Aroostook* and the *PN9–1*, which are described in the following text can be found in USS *Aroostook* unless otherwise noted. Rodgers's reaction, if any, to the bearings he received are taken from Rodgers Report.

32. Rodgers said in his postflight report, and on several other occasions, that he paid little or no attention to the radio bearings. His reason was "there had been no need of them, since all the station ships had been sighted without trouble and I did not feel it was necessary to frequently change course to pass the destroyers close aboard." Rodgers Report.

33. USS *Aroostook*; and USS *Farragut*.

34. The *Aroostook* had left station Vice at 1455 and was headed up the flight path to get nearer to the plane. She estimated that the *PN9–1* should come abeam station Vice at about 1525. USS *Aroostook*.

35. The *Aroostook* had stopped seven miles east of station Vice at 1530. They were now becoming worried that the *PN9–1* had already passed to the south of the ship without having been seen. Actually, the *PN9–1* had not yet reached the ship. Ibid.

36. The *Aroostook* also acted on the 181 degree bearing. "As bearings of 181 degrees and 247 degrees indicated the plane had probably passed [the] *Aroostook*, the course was changed to 240 degrees, true at 1555 . . . ." (The *Aroostook* was going back down the flight path and away from the *PN9–1*.) Ibid; and Rodgers Report.

37. USS *Aroostook*; and USS *Farragut*.

38. Ibid.

39. Rodgers Report.

40. Rodgers later wrote a letter of commendation praising the work done by the *Aroostook*. In the letter he attributed the bad bearings to interference. Captain Van Auken wrote in his report, "The operators state all signals from [the] *PN9–1* came in strong all the time notwithstanding much atmospheric and commercial interference." Rodgers Report; and USS *Aroostook*.

41. *New York Times*, 25 September 1925.

42. Associated Press as reported in the *San Jose Mercury Herald*, 8 September 1925.

False Hope, 1–3 September 1925

1. Associated Press as reported in the *San Jose Mercury Herald*, 1 September 1925.

2. Ibid.

3. Unless otherwise noted, the sources for the actions and state-

ments of the *PN9–1*'s crew are a series of exclusive postflight interviews given to the *New York Times*. The interviews appeared in the *New York Times*, 21–26 September 1925.

4. USS *Aroostook;* USS *Farragut.*

5. Stantz had copied all the radio traffic related to the search for, and rescue of, the *PN9–3*. He had passed this information on to his fellow crewmen. *New York Times*, 25 September 1925.

6. The basic color scheme used on the *PN9–1* was that which had become standard for naval aircraft on 29 May 1925. Her hull and wings were aluminum color and the top surfaces of the upper wings, stabilizers, and elevators were orange-yellow. In order to make her easily identifiable during the flight, the bow and the entire tail assembly had also been painted orange-yellow. Deputy Chief of Naval Operations (Air) and Commander, Naval Air System Command, *United States Naval Aviation 1910–1917*, p. 58; and Commander Flight Project, "Change in Instructions for the Flight," 10 August 1925. A4–3 (7–1).

7. Rodgers Report.

8. Rodgers's opinion was supported by the *Aroostook*'s postflight report. "It was not known for sure whether the plane was north or south of point V, but from progression of bearings it plotted south." USS *Aroostook.*

9. Associated Press as reported in the *San Jose Mercury Herald*, 2 September 1925; and *San Francisco Chronicle*, 2 September 1925.

10. Rodgers Report.

11. Gavin Report; Snody Report; and Associated Press as reported in the *San Jose Mercury Herald*, 3 September 1925.

12. USS *Aroostook;* USS *Farragut;* and USS *Tanager.*

13. Rodgers Report; and USS *Aroostook*, "Preliminary Report on Search Operations." 7 September 1925. (This report is different than the previous *Aroostook* report which has been cited. Hereafter this report will be cited as USS *Aroostook*-Search). A4–3 (7–1).

14. The sources describing the tow and capsizing of the *PN9–3* are the Snody Report; Gavin Report; and *San Francisco Chronicle*, 3 September 1925.

15. Earlier, the press had reassured the public that the *PN9–1* might still be afloat even if she were swamped. The report said, in part, "Experts pointed out that the gasoline tanks of the missing plane would have a buoyancy sufficient to float 10,855 pounds. The plane itself, without its fuel load weighs 9,100 pounds and the crew of five men would be less than 1,000 pounds." Associated Press as reported in the *San Jose Mercury Herald*, 3 September 1925.

16. On several occasions the planet Venus and the moon were

reported as flares by lookouts on the searching ships. USS *Aroostook-Search*.

17. John Toland, *The Great Dirigibles*, p. 103.

18. This was the opinion expressed by Rodgers in his postflight report. Rodgers Report.

19. Associated Press as reported in the *San Jose Mercury Herald*, 4 September 1925.

20. Today we would not describe an aircrash which took fourteen lives as a disaster as the crash of a single modern airplane could cause the deaths of several hundred people. But in 1925 air travel was a novelty and aviation news was nearly always reported sensationally. The public's attitude toward aviation and the fact that the *Shenandoah* was the first rigid airship built in the United States made her loss a national disaster.

21. Associated Press as reported in the *San Jose Mercury Herald*, 4 September 1925.

22. Ibid.

23. USS *Langley*, "Search for *PN9–1* by *Langley*," 17 September 1925. (This report is separate from the *Langley* report previously cited. Hereafter this report will be cited as USS *Langley*-Search.) A4–3 (7–1).

24. Rodgers Report.

25. USS *Aroostook*-Search; and USS *Farragut*.

26. USS *Aroostook*-Search.

27. USS *Aroostook*-Search; USS *Farragut* and USS *Whippoorwill*, "Report of Activities during West Coast-Hawaii Flight," 22 September 1925 (hereafter cited as USS *Whippoorwill*). A4–3 (7–1).

Determination and Despair, 4–7 September 1925

1. Associated Press as reported in the *San Jose Mercury Herald*, 4 September 1925.

2. Ibid.

3. USS *Aroostook*-Search.

4. Rodgers Report.

5. Ibid.

6. Ibid.

7. All actions and statements attributed to the *PN9–1*'s crew that are described in this chapter are taken from the *New York Times*, 21–26 September 1925 unless otherwise noted.

8. USS *Reno*.

9. Associated Press as reported in the *San Jose Mercury Herald*, 5 September 1925.

10. There is no specific source for this figure. The author's experience has been, however, that people planning to sail from San Francisco allow about nineteen days for the passage to Hawaii. Depending upon the wind conditions and the boats' size, some cross more quickly and others more slowly. But nineteen days is a good estimate.

11. Jim Gibbs, *West Coast Windjammers*, p. 42.

12. Lieutenant J. J. Hathaway, Letter, 28 October 1977. In the author's possession.

13. Captain Jackson strongly supported Captain Van Auken's conduct of the search. He specifically commended Van Auken for covering the Kauai Channel. USS *Langley*-Search.

14. The accounts of the drifting F–5L and the *Lynchburg* hoax are from Associated Press as reported in the *San Jose Mercury Herald*, 5 September 1925.

15. Rodgers Report.

16. Ibid.

17. USS *Langley*-Search.

18. The newspaper account of Mitchell's statement is found in Associated Press as reported in the *San Jose Mercury Herald*, 6 September 1925. (The entire text of General Mitchell's statement was printed in the paper).

19. Ibid.

20. Ibid.

21. Rodgers Report.

22. Ibid.

23. USS *Aroostook*-Search.

24. USS *Farragut*.

25. USS *Reno*.

26. USS *Aroostook*-Search.

27. USS *Farragut*.

28. Associated Press as reported in the *San Jose Mercury Herald*, 7 September 1925.

29. USS *Aroostook*-Search.

30. The *Langley* and her pilots used the opportunity afforded by the search operations to develop and test many of their scouting techniques and flying skills. Captain Jackson commented on one such experiment. "A noteworthy feat was that accomplished by Lieutenant Flagg of VF–2. By premeditation he landed and brought his plane to rest in the middle of the deck near the elevator where the arresting gear was not rigged. He was at the time making a practice pass over the deck. His engine was idling when he came to rest. Wind about thirty-three miles over the deck. Said he had always wanted to try it. He was

admonished not to attempt this again as it is considered too dangerous a procedure for peace times." USS *Langley*-Search.

31. USS *Aroostook*-Search.

32. Rodgers Report.

33. Ibid; and M. B. McComb, "Report of Damage and Repairs to *PN9–1*, A6838," 24 September 1925. A4–3 (7–1).

34. USS *Langley*-Search.

35. Ibid.

36. USS *Aroostook*-Search.

Rescue, 8–10 September 1925

1. Associated Press as reported in the *San Jose Mercury Herald*, 8 September 1925.

2. Rodgers Report.

3. All actions and statements attributed to the crew are taken from the postflight interviews which appeared in the *New York Times*, 21–26 September 1925.

4. John Rodgers, "Navy Day Address," 27 October 1925, RFP.

5. John Rodgers, "Speech to the National Aeronautical Association."

6. The source of the flares was never explained, but this sighting was not one which was attributed to Venus or the moon. USS *Langley*-Search.

7. "The planes were called in after two hours search with a view to conserving them, inasmuch as the same areas were to be searched later. . . . Subsequent information shows that the "Fortunes of War" probably hinged on this decision . . . . They apparently were, at the end of their search, exceedingly close to the missing plane; and might have picked it up at any minute thereafter." USS *Langley*-Search.

8. Commander Submarines Pearl Harbor, "Submarine Movements in Connection with Search for *PN9–1*," 17 September 1925 (hereafter cited as Commander Submarines). A4–3 (7–1).

9. USS *Langley*-Search.

10. Associated Press as reported in the *San Jose Mercury Herald*, 10 September 1925.

11. Commandant 14th Naval District, "Search Operations for Lost Seaplane *PN9–1*," 17 September 1925, RFP.

12. USS *Langley*-Search.

13. Commander Submarines.

14. Deck log, USS *R–4*, 10 September 1925. (Hereafter cited as Deck log, R–4).

15. *Kansas City Star*, 20 July 1926. (Osborn, who was visiting his parents, was interviewed by a *Star* reporter.)

16. There are two versions of this refusal. Rodgers reportedly said that having gone this far they were not going to quit now. He added that staying with the plane would mean that upon reaching the harbor the flight would be, technically, complete. The other, which comes from Osborn, is that Rodgers refused on the grounds that the entire crew was needed to handle the plane. There is probably truth to both versions. Out of this refusal, there grew a minor myth. During post-rescue interviews several crew members said that the arrival of the *R–4* was something of a disappointment. They did not want to be rescued; they wanted to sail into harbor themselves. One press account said that the rescue deprived the airmen of the satisfaction of sailing into harbor on their own. Only their sense of duty made them accept the tow. Rodgers's version and the myth are found in an AP release printed in the *San Jose Mercury Herald*, 15 September 1925; and the *New York Times*, 26 September 1925. Rodgers's account is found in the Rodgers Report and Osborn's version was reported in the *Kansas City Star*, 20 July 1926.

17. *Kansas City Star*, 20 July 1926.

18. Ibid; and M. B. McComb, "Report of Damage and Repair to *PN9–1*, 24 September 1925. A4–3 (7–1).

19. Deck log, *R–4*; and Rodgers Report.

20. The account of the *PN9–1*'s trials and tribulations which started after she was cast off from the *R–4* are taken from Rodgers Report and the *New York Times*, 21–26 September 1925.

Epilogue

1. *Farragut* Report.

2. *Aroostook* Report.

3. Captain E. S. Jackson, the *Langley*'s captain, was even more specific about the lack of information regarding the *PN9–1*'s position. He felt that the guard vessels and the plane had failed to adequately provide this vital information throughout the flight. His comments on this aspect of the flight fill one single-spaced typed page. USS *Langley*.

4. Walter Millis, ed., *American Military Thought*, p. 374.

5. Ibid., pg. 397.

6. Associated Press as reported in the *San Jose Mercury Herald*, 11–12 September 1925.

7. Ibid.

8. Aircraft record cards A–6799 and A–6878, Reference Library,

National Air and Space Museum, Smithsonian Institution, Washington, D.C.

9. Material Division, Memorandum "PB–2 Airplane," 19 October 1932; 1st endorsement, 25 October 1932; and approved by RAdm. W. A. Moffett, 25 October 1932, BURAERO General Correspondence, 1925–1942 file VPB1/F1–1, Old Army and Navy Branch, National Archives, Washington, D.C.

10. *New York Times*, 22 September 1925.

11. The events surrounding Rodgers's death are found in "Records of Proceedings of a Board of Inquest in the case of John Rodgers, late Commander U.S. Navy," 27 August 1926; and "Record of Proceedings of a Board of Investigation to Inquire into and report upon the Crashing of Airplane of Commander John Rodgers," 28 August 1926, Record Group 125, Case Nr. 14306.

Bibliography

Manuscripts

Bureau of Aeronautics File A4–3 (7–1). Navy and Old Army Branch. National Archives, Washington, D.C.

Deck log USS *R–4*. Navy and Old Army Branch. National Archives, Washington, D.C.

John Rodgers' Speech to the Aeronautical Association, 9 October 1925. Naval Historical Center, Washington, D.C.

"The Navy Pacific Flight." Undated. Excerpts from Rodgers' Speech to the National Aeronautical Association in New York, 9 October 1925. Naval Historical Center, Washington, D.C.

Record Group 80. Navy and Old Army Branch. National Archives, Washington, D.C.

Record Group 125. Records of the Judge Advocate General (Navy), National Archives, Washington, D.C.

The Rodgers Family Papers. Library of Congress, Washington, D.C.

"Rodgers' Flight to Hawaii." Aviation History Unit File Copy, 1945, Naval Historical Center, Washington, D.C.

Newspapers

The *Kansas City Star*, 1926. Kansas City.

The *New York Times*, 1924–1926. New York.

The *San Diego Union*, 1925. San Diego.

The *San Francisco Chronicle*, 1925. San Francisco.

The *San Jose Mercury Herald*, 1925. San Jose.

Periodicals and Magazines

Naval Aviation News, 1974. Washington, D.C.

The Airpower Historian, 1961. Maxwell, Alabama AFB.

U.S. Naval Institute *Proceedings*, 1965. Annapolis, Maryland.

General Works

Bowers, Peter. *Boeing Aircraft Since 1916*. Fallbrook, Cal.: Aero Publishers, 1966.

Chief of Naval Operations, Naval History Division. *United States Naval Aviation, 1910–1970*. Washington, D.C.: Government Printing Office, 1970.

Dickey, Phillips S. *The Liberty Engine 1918–1942*. Washington, D.C.: Smithsonian Press, 1968.

Gibbs, Jim. *West Coast Windjammers*. New York: Bonanza, 1958.

Horvat, William. *Above the Pacific*. Fallbrook, Cal.: Aero Publishers, 1966.

Howeth, L. S. *History of Communications-Electronics in the United States Navy*. Washington, D.C.: Government Printing Office, 1963.

Jordanoff, Assen. *Jordanoff's Illustrated Aviation Dictionary*. New York: Collier and Son, 1942.

Mason, Herbert M. *The United States Air Force: A Turbulent History*. New York: Charter, 1976.

Millis, Walter. *American Military Thought*. New York, Indianapolis and Kansas City: Bobs-Merrill Co., 1966.

Mitchell, William. *Winged Defense*. New York and London: Putnam's Sons, 1925.

Nye, Willis L. *Metal Aircraft: Design and Construction*. San Francisco: Aviation Press, 1935.

Page, Victor W. *Modern Aviation Engines*. Vol. 2. New York: Henley Publishing Co., 1929.

Schlaifer, Robert. *Development of Aircraft Engines*. Andover, Massachusetts: Andover Press, 1950.

Smith, Richard K. *First Across*. Annapolis, Maryland: Naval Institute Press, 1973.

Stinton, Darrol. *The Anatomy of the Aeroplane*. New York: American Publishing Co., 1966.

Swanborough, Gordon and Bowers, Peter. *U.S. Navy Aircraft Since 1911*. London: Putnam's Sons, 1968.

Toland, John. *The Great Dirigibles*. New York: Dover, 1972.

Turnball, Archibald D. and Lord Clifford L. *History of United States Naval Aviation*. New Haven: Yale University Press, 1949.

Wagner, Russell F. *History of the United States Army*. New York: Macmillian Co., 1967.

Wilson, Eugene E. *Slipstream*. Palm Beach: Literary Investment Guild, 1967.

Index